RETENTION OF TITLE CLAUSES IN SALE OF GOODS CONTRACTS IN EUROPE

Contents

First published 1999 by Ashgate Publishing

2 Park Square, Milton Park, Abingdon, Oxfordshire OX14 4RN
52 Vanderbilt Avenue, New York, NY 10017

Routledge is an imprint of the Taylor & Francis Group, an informa business

First issued in paperback 2020

British Library Cataloguing in Publication Data
Retention of title clauses in sale of goods contracts in
Europe
1.Sales, Conditional - European Union countries
I.Davies, Iwan II.Association of European Lawyers
341.7'54'094

Library of Congress Cataloging-in-Publication Data
Retention of title clauses in sale of goods contracts in Europe /
editor ; Iwan Davies.
p. cm.

1. Sales, Conditional--Europe. 2. Priorities of claims and liens--Europe. 3. Debtor and creditor--Europe. I. Davies, Iwan.
KJC1291.R48 1999
346.407'4--dc21 99-25793
CIP

ISBN 13: 978-0-7546-2008-2 (hbk)
ISBN 13: 978-0-367-60505-6 (pbk)

Retention of Title Clauses in Sale of Goods Contracts in Europe

Edited by
IWAN DAVIES
Centre for Instalment Credit Law
University of Wales, Swansea

ROUTLEDGE
Routledge
Taylor & Francis Group
LONDON AND NEW YORK

Editorial

PETER KAYE, GENERAL SERIES EDITOR

This series of volumes to be produced as part of the European Legal Practitioner project by members of the Faculty of Law of the University of Wales Swansea in collaboration with the *Association of European Lawyers* is intended to provide a useful bridge between academic and practical approaches to selected fields of legal activities.

The distinction between 'academic' and 'practical', in any event somewhat less pronounced on the Continent of Europe than is traditionally the case in the United Kingdom, grows ever narrower in those areas of law where drafting and procedural steps must pay close and constant attention to the developed theory and jurisprudence of the subject; whilst, conversely, today's academic theory can rarely afford to ignore the practical implications of its proposals.

Hence the mission of the series: to furnish succinct accounts of different countries' laws in particular areas, which amount as far as possible to a description of the actual conditions and practical operation of the law and are thereby of immediate use to those in practice, as well as being of additional value to scholars involved in the comparative analysis of European laws.

The series begins with Professor Iwan Davies' editorship of the drafting of retention of title clauses, which itself perfectly exemplifies the desired marriage between theory and practice for the overall concern of the modern European legal practitioner.

Swansea, although only a small and recently established law faculty, nevertheless views this series of volumes as a particularly appropriate contribution for it to make at the present stage, in view of its specialisation in international civil and commercial law, and further volumes in the series are currently at the preparatory stage.

Faculty of Law
University of Wales, Swansea

Peter Kaye
Professor of Private
International and European Law

Editor's Preface

A characteristic of sale of goods contracts is the mutuality of promises made between the seller and buyer whereby the former promises to deliver the goods and the buyer in return promises to pay the purchase price. In practical terms the purchaser is often unable to pay the purchase price to the seller unless he has had the opportunity to sell the goods to his customer, or perhaps deal with them in such a way including subjecting them to a manufacturing process so as to generate proceeds out of which the buyer will pay the original seller. The purpose of a retention of title clause is to secure the position of the seller where delivery of goods has taken place without payment having been made. Essentially, it is a contractual stipulation whereby the seller defers the transfer of property in the goods to the fulfilment of the primary obligations under the contract most notably, payment of the price. As such, the passing of property in the goods is aspect of contract rather than conveyance or delivery.

In this series of essays retention of title clauses can be seen as a European phenomenon. What clearly emerges is that the extent of the recognition of the validity of such clauses and the formal requirements for establishing such clauses varies greatly from jurisdiction to jurisdiction. The framework for such clauses can be identified as follows: first the primary clause reserving title to goods *in specie*; second, horizontal extensions into debts; third, vertical extensions which seek to follow the goods supplied into a finished product or its proceeds. The profusion of such clauses in Europe may indicate a symptom of the law's inability in each jurisdiction to protect trade creditors. As Tepora has argued:

> "The use of reservation of title *(reservatio dominii)* implies a reliance, through the incorporation of a proviso on the right of ownership, on the set of norms regulating rights of ownership, and on the corresponding legal conception of right of ownership in cases where legislation has not provided any appropriate methods of satisfying the needs in question." [1]

---

[1] Tepora, J. "Reservation of Title as Security and in the Administration of Property" (1985) 29 *Scandinavian Studies in Law* 213.

The policy question posed by such clauses is the extent to which they adequately solve the practical problems which emerge in the sale of goods process including the conflicting rights of the creditors of the buyer and seller in addition to those of the good faith purchaser. There are at least two narrow legal issues which arise in this context: first, whether a reservation of title clause should prevail against a good faith purchaser from the buyer; second, whether the clause should be good against the buyer's creditors. What emerges from these essays is that the response to these issues depend upon the underlying legal framework in each jurisdiction and may even vary dependent upon the nature of the goods in question.

Reservation of title clauses in contracts for the sale of goods are not affected by the Uniform Law on the International Sale of Goods[2] nor the Vienna Convention on International Sales Law.[3] Whilst in most of the jurisdictions examined in this series of essays the accepted principle of private international law is that contractual obligations are governed by the proper law of the contract, nonetheless, the contract's effects in the law of property are determined by the *lex rei sitae*. What emerges is that there is no uniform approach to the recognition of such clauses.

On the assumption that the creation of effective security interests bolsters the supply of credit[4] the need for a European uniform approach to retention of title clauses is self-evident, that is, setting out the extent of the law's protection to unpaid trade creditors of goods. Since the draft Directive in 1980[5] not much progress has been made within the European Union in harmonising the recognition of retention of title clauses within the Member States. Significantly under the draft Directive[6] on late payments in commercial transactions between enterprises in the private sector and between such enterprises and the public sector, Member States are required to take the appropriate steps to ensure that national legislation

---

2 Article 8.

3 Article 4 (b).

4 See Goode RM, "Transcending the Boundaries of Earth and Space: The Preliminary Draft UNIDROIT Convention on International Interests in Mobile Equipment" [1998] *Uniform Law Review 52.*

5 Working Paper 111/D/278/80.

6 OJ 1998 No C168/98.

contains provisions according to which the seller can retain title to the goods sold until the buyer has made payment and be able to recover them until payment has been made. As the European Union expands and trade increases between Member States the time may have come to reconsider more fully the issue of a uniform approach to retention of title clauses within Europe as this would simplify the use and enforcement of these clauses in such trade.

It is entirely appropriate for me to thank the contributors to this Volume who are, in the main, members of the Association of European Lawyers. In particular I would like to thank Bruce Burniston of Morgan Cole, Solicitors, for his unfailing enthusiasm, patience and support for the Project.

Faculty of Law
University of Wales, Swansea

Iwan Davies
Professor of Law
Centre for Instalment Credit Law

Note on Contributors

Lotte Vilandt Agerbaek is a practising lawyer with Plesner and Gronborg, Copenhagen, Denmark.

Alfonso Areitio is a practising lawyer at Gomez Acebo and Pombo, Madrid, Spain.

Knut Bachke is a practising lawyer with Bull and Co, Oslo, Norway.

Gerard Carriere is a practising lawyer with Nauta Dutilh, Rotterdam, Holland.

Iwan Davies is a practising barrister and Professor of Law at the Centre for Instalment and Credit Law, University of Wales, Swansea.

Alvise Donà dalle Rose is a practising lawyer at Piergrossi Villa Manca Graziadei, Milan, Italy.

Sebastian Jägerhorn is a practising lawyer with Hannes Snellman, Helsinki, Finland.

Philipp Känzig is a practising lawyer with Staiger, Schwald and Roesle, Zurich, Switzerland.

Mats Koffner is a practising lawyer with Advokatfirman Glimstedt, Gottenburg, Sweden.

Rui Peixoto Duarte is a practising lawyer at Dr Rui Peixoto Duarte Law Offices, Porto, Portugal.

Magnus Pousette is a practising lawyer with Hannes Snellman, Helsinki, Finland.

Marc Saint-Cène is a practising lawyer at Courtois Lebel and Associates, Paris, France.

Friedrich Schwank is a practising lawyer at the Law Offices of Dr F. Schwank, Vienna, Austria.

Costas Vainanidis is a practising lawyer at Vainanidis Schina and Economou, Athens, Greece.

Nicole Van Crombrugghe is a practising lawyer at Lafili, Van Crombrugghe and Partners, Brussels, Belgium.

Bernd Waas is a Senior Research Fellow at the University of Trier, Germany.

The Association of European Lawyers

The Association of European Lawyers ("AEL") was created in 1989 with the object of providing readily available expert legal services in English across Europe. Originally established by the compiling of resources of five leading law firms in the UK, a non-exclusive network of correspondent firms throughout Europe has been developed, offering a broad range of legal services for business, with high standards of care and efficiency.

The objectives of AEL can be summarised as follows:-

- the provision of integrated legal services to businesses across the whole of Europe
- the maintenance of the highest standards of client care and professional expertise
- the development of non-exclusive links between member firms for information exchange and training.

The advantages of AEL are that each member firm:-

- has rapid and direct access to the services of other members
- knows the individuals in other member firms, leading to close and harmonious working relationships to the benefit of the client
- can have confidence in the high professional standards of the other members
- agrees to follow a code of conduct when providing the service to a client.

Since 1989 AEL has held training and general meetings on a variety of commercial legal subjects, and in 1997 its training seminar on commercial joint ventures, held in Madrid, was awarded funding from the European Commission under the GROTIUS programme.

Continually expanding, it currently has 36 members covering the European Union, Eastern Europe, the Baltic States and Cyprus.

1 Austria

FRIEDRICH SCHWANK

Introduction

The sale of goods on credit allows the buyer to obtain actual possession and use of the goods prior to the payment of the purchase price. In order to reduce the buyer's insolvency risk to the seller the latter may seek to retain title to the goods until the purchase price has been paid notwithstanding that delivery has taken place. Though not specifically regulated in the Austrian General Civil Code or in the Commercial Code, a retention of title clause is a popular and frequently used device by sellers when delivering goods on credit. To be effective the retention of title clause requires an agreement between both the seller and the buyer and a unilateral retention of title clause is legally ineffective.[1] Consent may be given expressly or may be implied by the actions of the buyer such as the unconditional acceptance of the possession of the goods sold subject to the clause.

The legal position of the buyer in respect to goods sold subject to a retention of title clause is characterised by his right to possess and use the goods including the right of *usufruct*. Even though the buyer does not enjoy full ownership rights, nonetheless, he has an action in Austrian law to defend his possession of the goods against third parties on the basis of the purchase price. Furthermore where the goods are damaged the buyer has an action for damages against the tortfeasor notwithstanding the action of the seller as owner of the goods.[2]

Retention of Title Clause: The Legal Background

With the exception of consumer contracts and contracts involving plant and equipment there are no particular formal requirements for retention of title clauses under Austrian law. In the case of hire purchase contracts involving consumers, the terms of such an agreement have to be recorded

---

1 Austrian Supreme Court decisions published in ÖBA, 1987, 51 and RdW 1987, 157.

2 Austrian Supreme Court decisions published in SZ 51/164, JBL 1980, 262.

in writing including any reservation of title clause.[3] Where this does not occur, the seller is exposed to the potential sanction of a fine and also a desist action for unfair competition but the agreement is not treated as a nullity. In the case of plant and equipment sales, if the reservation of title clause has not been recorded in the land registry the plant or equipment will be considered as part and parcel of the land and the owner of the land recorded in the land registry will be deemed to have a good title in the plant and equipment.[4] In all other sales of goods contracts whilst there is no requirement that a retention of title clause must be in writing this will obviously be relevant for the purpose of evidentiary considerations and, in practice, most such clauses are in writing.

The form of retention of title

For the purposes of Austrian law a simple reservation of title clause will read as follows: "The seller retains title to the goods sold until the purchase price has been paid in full and on time". Often there will be other provisions, for example, an undertaking by the buyer to look after the goods carefully, to store them and insure them against all possible risks. Insofar as the more extended clauses are concerned where sub-sale is anticipated, there are two ways to deal with this phenomenon under Austrian law: first, substitution of the goods sold to the proceeds of sale; second, extending retention of title to the second buyer. Each of these will now be considered in turn.

The substitution of the goods sold by the proceeds of sale requires careful drafting. In addition to the simple reservation of title clause the following should be included: "[T]he buyer is entitled to resell the goods subject to the condition that the proceeds of such sale are being paid directly by the second buyer into an escrow account in favour of the original seller retaining title to the goods". The payment of the proceeds into a separate escrow account is required in order to be able to identify the separate ownership of the original seller in respect of the proceeds. If this is not done then the original seller will not be able to claim title to the proceeds as the funds will have been mixed and neither will the original seller be able to recover the goods where the sub-buyer has acted in good faith. The other method of passing down the reservation of title clause requires an agreement between the first buyer agreeing with the second

---

3 Article 21 (1) Consumer Protection Act.

4 Article 297a General Civil Code.

buyer in turn that the reservation of title clause in favour of the original seller is being passed down to the second buyer. The first buyer assigns to the second buyer his right to obtain valid title to the goods upon full and timely payment of the purchase price. The second buyer will have to pay the original seller directly in order to obtain a good title.

In the case of more extended clauses to goods manufactured from material supplied by the seller to the buyer subject to a retention of title clause, the general position under Austrian law is that the seller will lose the retained title to the goods if they have lost their identity and cannot be severed from the finished product. In some circumstances it might be possible to agree that the seller becomes a co-owner of any goods manufactured by the buyer. However, this will not only require an appropriate agreement between the parties but also some form of transfer of the title of the newly manufactured goods of the buyer back to the original seller. In contrast where bulk commodities are sold subject to a reservation of title clause, the seller may agree with the buyer that he becomes a co-owner of such bulk commodities provided the goods are stored in such a manner that the ownership quota of the original seller can easily be identified.

Effects of retention of title outside insolvency

In the absence of voluntary co-operation by the buyer, the seller is not allowed to enforce the retention of title clause against the buyer without recourse to law and the assistance of the court. In order to protect his position against unauthorised sub-sale it is prudent for the original seller to label by way of a notice the goods delivered to the effect that they are subject to a retention of title clause and in this way it may be possible to argue that the sub-buyer is not in good faith where the original buyer wrongfully sells the goods on to him. In any event, in the case of plant or equipment it is necessary to register the retention of title clause in the appropriate land registry because otherwise the plant or equipment will be treated as being part and parcel of the property where the facility is situated.

In cases of immovable property, rights on such immovable property, ships, patents, trademarks and designs, the registration in a land registry or another public register is full evidence of the title. The passing of the title of ownership from seller to buyer takes place by amending the register. Ownership to all other movable property is not capable of being recorded in a public register under Austrian law. The actual possession of such movable property is in the ordinary course of events a sign of ownership in respect of which *bona fide* third parties can rely upon and acquire a good title in the goods.

Where the buyer is in default, the seller can request the return of the goods. Such a request is categorised, in the absence of a contrary agreement,[5] as a rescission of the purchase contract. In the alternative the seller may seek to recover from the buyer by way of an action for payment of the purchase price. If the seller subsequently uses the judgment against the buyer for purposes of enforcing his claim by way of attaching the goods sold, it is assumed that by so doing the seller has waived his reservation of title clause.[6]

Retention of title clauses within the local insolvency regime

A valid retention of title clause remains effective in the insolvency of the buyer as such goods will be excluded from the insolvent's estate. The court appointed administrator or trustee is under a duty to return the goods subject to such a clause unless the goods have been sub-sold or they have been mixed with other goods. Of course the seller's claim to title will be subject to scrutiny on the basis of fraudulent preference. In this respect reservation of title clauses are liable to be challenged if they have been created retrospectively, that is, in circumstances where title has been re-transferred to the seller when the buyer was unable to pay the purchase price timeously as provided for by the contract.

Private international law considerations

Austrian conflict of law rules are codified in the Act on International Private law (IPRG). The legal position under this legislation is that the loss of rights to tangible assets is always governed by the *lex rei sitae*. Thus, the validity and enforceability of a retention of title clause will be governed by the law where the assets are situated.[7] A reservation of title clause validly agreed abroad under foreign law will be accepted as valid under Austrian law so long as the goods are abroad and are subject to the foreign law. However, as soon as the goods are brought into Austria a

---

5 Supreme Court decisions published in SZ 55/152, JBL 1986, 307.

6 Supreme Court decisions published in SZ 24/91, SZ 40/50, SZ 57/192.

7 Article 31 (1) IPRG.

foreign retention of title clause may not be enforceable to the extent that third party rights are affected. Further, it should be noted that Austrian conflict of law rules contain additional special provisions in respect of certain transport vehicles. Thus, the title to water or sea-borne vehicles is subject to the law of the state of registration. In respect of railway rolling-stock, the law of the state to be applied is that of where the operating railway company has its administrative headquarters.[8] All other vehicles including cars are subject to the general Austrian conflict of law rules.

---

[8] Article 33 (1) IPRG.

2 Belgium

NICOLE VAN CROMBRUGGHE

Introduction

Under Belgian law, the sale of goods contract is considered to be perfected as soon as the parties have reached an agreement as to price and the subject-matter of the contract.[1] It follows from this that title of the asset sold passes with immediate effect at the conclusion of the contract without delivery having taken place. Even so, the unpaid seller is offered a number of remedies under Belgian law: first, the seller can refuse to deliver the goods (*excepito non adimpleti contractus*);[2] second, the seller can rescind the contract in the absence of a judicial settlement;[3] third, where delivery has taken place pursuant to a non-credit sale and payment is not forthcoming, the seller is entitled to repossession provided this takes place within eight days following delivery and the item is still in its original state;[4] fourth, notwithstanding the term of the contract in respect of payment the seller will enjoy a lien over the goods so long as they are in their original state and have not become fixtures.[5]

The parties to a sale of goods contract can agree to delay the transfer of title notwithstanding that delivery has taken place. The nature of the clause recognised under Belgian law is a simple one, that is, the seller continues to enjoy ownership of the goods until payment for those goods has been made in full. In the absence of a trade custom, for example, as exists in the diamond trade sector, it is necessary for a reservation of title to be specifically inserted in the contract of sale and in the absence of this no such provision is normally implied.

---

1 Article 1593, Civil Code.
2 Article 1612, Civil Code.
3 Article 21, Judicial Settlement Act.
4 Article 20, 5 para.6, Mortgage Act.
5 Specific rules are provided in favour of the seller of industrial equipment.

Retention of Title Clauses: The Legal Background

There are no specific formalities required. This is in stark contrast to the creation of a lien in favour of the seller of industrial property which requires the corresponding invoice to be filed with the registrar of the court at the purchaser's domicile no later than 15 days after the delivery. Compliance with this formality will authorise the seller to uphold his lien for a period of five years after delivery even if the asset has become a fixture or the buyer has been declared bankrupt so long as the asset has remained in the possession of the buyer. In the context of bankruptcy, however, a retention of title clause must be evidenced in writing at the latest by the time the goods are delivered[6] if this is to be enforced against the buyer.

In enforcement proceedings the buyer must be informed of the seller's decision in this respect and the seller must comply with the contractual stipulations regulating this. An automatic rescission clause is often included in sales contracts together with a reservation of title clause. There is no conceptual difficulty here and indeed Article 1184 of the Civil Code provides that a party faced with a breach of contract committed by his contracting party is entitled as a matter of law to claim rescission of the contract. From a tactical perspective the advantage of providing for an express rescissionary provision is that the parties can determine precisely the circumstances amounting to a breach of contract without the need for the intervention of the court. Nonetheless there is an important limitation, namely, a clause which provides for automatic rescission of the contract where the buyer applies for or obtains a judicial settlement is deemed to be unenforceable by virtue of Article 28 Judicial Settlement Act.

It is often the case in practice that where repossession of the goods occurs this will require garnishment by way of *saisie-revendication.* This amounts to a protective measure enabling the owner to obtain the appointment of a custodian with whom the asset in question will be placed pending the decision in respect of the merits of the matter having been made.

[6] Article 106 Bankruptcy Act.

Judicial Settlement

All the remedies available to creditors including retention of title are suspended during a period determined by the court (subject to a maximum of six months) following an application being made for a Judicial Settlement. During this period the applicant is obliged to prepare a recovery plan which must include those items which are covered by a retention of title clause. The plan may provide that the enforcement of such a clause should not occur as this would be in conflict with the continuation of the applicant's business. In that case, specific provision must be made in the plan for the payment of interest in respect of the sums owed under the retention of title clause and, in any event, payment may not be delayed for more than an 18 month period. If any of these conditions are not met, the seller's consent will be required.

Bankruptcy

Except in circumstances where the law provides otherwise, all creditors rank equally and the *pari passu* principle of distribution applies so that when the debtor's assets are insufficient to pay all the creditors in full, the proceeds will be divided among the creditors in proportion to their respective claim. The issue of preference under Belgian law is strictly determined and is restricted to liens and mortgages including security interests in specific assets of the debtor.[7] At the same time preferential mechanisms are also available, notably the insertion of a clause providing for rescission of the contract of sale on the occurrence of certain identified events.

---

[7] Special provision is made under Belgian law in respect of non-consumer finance leasing contracts by virtue of the Royal decree No.55, November 10, 1967 and further implemented by Ministerial Decrees of February 23, 1968 and December 24, 1976. Provided the operation qualifies as being "finance leasing" (which requires the rent to be calculated on the basis of the presumed duration of the economic life of the asset and the contract *includes* a purchase option) the owner/lessor can repossess the equipment even where the debtor/lessee is subject to bankruptcy proceedings or subject to a judicial settlement. However, it should be noted that specific approval from the Ministry of Economic Affairs is necessary to conduct finance leasing operations.

An important change to Belgian law was occasioned by the Bankruptcy Act 1997. Article 101 of that Act explicitly recognises the validly of the retention of title clause in the bankruptcy of the buyer[8] so long as the following conditions are satisfied: first, the clause must be evidenced in writing at the latest by the time of delivery of the goods; second, the goods must be in possession of the buyer in their original state and have not become fixtures; third, the repossession claim must be made before the court has determined the claims filed in respect of the bankrupt's estate (*procès-verbal de vérification des créances*). It should be noted that the trustee in bankruptcy with the approval of the court might refuse the enforcement of a retention of title clause under Article 101 provided it is in the interest of the other creditors and the agreed price including interest is paid by the trustee to the seller.

Private International Law

The validity of a reservation of title clause is governed in accordance with the Hague Convention of June 15, 1955 by the law chosen by the parties and, in the absence of this, by the law of the country of residence of either the seller or purchaser. In respect of sales to consumers, the rules enacted by the Convention of Rome prevails so that in the absence of the parties electing the applicable law the law of the usual residence of the consumer buyer shall apply.

In the absence of an agreement among the creditors of the buyer, enforcement of a reservation of title clause is governed by the *lex rei sitae*. Classically the enforcement of such a clause will require it to be valid pursuant to the *lex contractus* and the limits set under the *lex rei sitae* to protect third parties have not been infringed. Difficulties may therefore arise under Belgian law in respect of the enforceability of an extended retention of title clause which offends the provisions of Article 2279 of the Civil Code, according to which "*en fait de meubles, possession vaut titre*".

---

8 Under the old law, Article 546 Bankruptcy Act 1851, the unpaid seller lost the benefit of a retention of title clause on the bankruptcy of the buyer.

3 Denmark

LOTTE VILANDT AGERBAEK

Introduction

Unless otherwise agreed it follows under the Danish Sale of Goods Act that upon delivery of the goods to the buyer the sale is complete from the point of view of the seller. This is so even though the buyer fails to fulfil the payment terms in accordance with the contract thereby compromising the position of the seller. In an attempt to avoid this conclusion the seller will often seek to protect his position through a retention of title mechanism.

Conditional sales in Denmark are, in large measure, regulated by the Danish Credit Agreements Act which, as well as stipulating a number of terms and conditions in respect of credit agreements in general also contains a number of provisions dealing with the validity of retention of title clauses. Under s.6 (1) of the Credit Agreements Act a conditional sale is defined as a purchase on credit in which the parties have agreed that the seller may repossess the delivered object if the buyer fails to fulfil his payment obligation. In terms of scope s.34 (3) of the Credit Agreements Act limits retention of title clauses to one purchase agreement and thereby outlaws overcollateralisation by adding new purchases to the old agreement. Further s.38 limits the amount which may be secured by a retention of title clause to: firstly, the unpaid part of the total debt relating to the goods sold; secondly, interest on payments already due relating to the goods sold; thirdly, necessary costs arising from the repossession of the object including collection charges. Subsequent costs in respect of repairs and maintenance to the object are not covered by the retention of title clause.

The Validity of Retention of Title Clauses

In order for a retention of title clause to be valid s.34 of the Credit Agreements Act set out the following requirements: first, the retention of title clause must have been agreed at the latest upon delivery of the goods; second, the total amount payable must exceed a minimum amount; third, the purchase on credit must not have taken place according to a credit agreement with a variable loan amount; fourth, the seller upon delivery of the goods has received payment of at least 20 per cent of the cash price. These requirements will now be discussed in turn.

The need for agreement and contract formalities

Section 34(1)(2) of the Credit Agreements Act makes it a condition that a retention of title clause has been agreed between the parties and that this meets certain criteria in respect of clearness and understanding. Further, the retention of title clause must be validly incorporated into the sale contract and must be specifically brought to the attention of the purchaser. It is not therefore sufficient for the seller to merely include a retention of title clause on an invoice and in any event, the invoice will often by post-contractual.

A retention of title clause cannot be imposed unilaterally by the seller. The purchaser must have accepted this condition in agreeing to purchase the goods. A dispute will often arise where the seller in the agreement or the order confirmation has made a reference to his normal business terms or to standard terms drawn up by a trade organisation. Such terms will not be incorporated unless they are expressly brought to the buyer's attention.[1] Thus, if the terms are stipulated in small letters on the back of the order form it is generally required that the letters are highlighted immediately above the purchaser's signature. If the purchaser has signed such a contract, the content of the contract is binding notwithstanding the fact that the purchaser claims that he was not familiar with the clause. In construing such a clause the approach adopted by the court is to construe it strictly against the seller who is relying upon it.

Section 34(1)(1) of the Credit Agreements Act provides that a retention of title clause is only valid if it is agreed between the parties at the latest upon delivery of the goods, that is, the goods are situated at the purchaser's or his representative's place of business or home. However the issue of delivery is a question of law and much depends upon the capacity in which the purchaser had possession of the goods, for example, if the goods are delivered on trial or are leant to the purchaser it is sufficient if

---

1 In determining the issue of notice whether such a term is normally incorporated into such business contracts is relevant as is the question of the length of business relationship between the parties and the terms upon which this relationship is based.

the retention of title clause is entered into by the time the buyer has adopted the transaction by agreeing to buy the goods.[2]

Retention of title and minimum payment amounts. Section 34(1)(2) stipulates a minimum purchase price must be agreed. At present the total amount payable must exceed DKK 2000. The total amount payable is a total of the principal, the down payment and the credit costs.[3]

Retention of title and variable loan amounts. According to s.34(1)(3) of the Credit Agreements Act, the retention of title cannot effectively be entered into if the purchase on credit takes place according to a credit agreement with a variable loan amount, for example a credit line. By a credit line a specifically stated credit amount is made available to the debtor who can draw amounts within this credit scheme.

Retention of title and minimum down payment. By virtue of s.34(1)(4) of the Credit Agreements Act in the case of a sale *to consumers*[4] it is a condition of the validity of a retention of title clause that the seller will have received 20 per cent of the cash price. Section 9(2) of the Act defines this to be the price at which the goods upon entering into an agreement could have been purchased in cash and the seller must not grant any credit to the buyer in respect of that part of the down payment. The minimum payment must be made before delivery. Some problems have emerged in valuing goods which are taken in part exchange in respect of the 20 per cent rule although it appears that a retention of title will not be set aside if the estimated fixed value is reasonable, even if it subsequently turns out that the total actual value of the down payment does not amount to 20 per cent of the cash price. Nevertheless the 20 per cent of cash price criterion is taken literally and it is well established that the retention of title is not valid if this condition has not been fulfilled even it is a question of an

---

2 See *U 1979. 430 V.* In this case the seller delivered cattle to a farmer in the last half of December 1979 giving him a right to inspect the cattle and reject those which he did not find suitable. Immediately following the last delivery on December 29 a contract was entered into containing a retention of title clause regarding the cattle already delivered. It was held that the retention of title clause was nevertheless valid.

3 S.9 (1) (3) Credit Agreements Act.

4 The minimum down payment condition is limited to consumer purchases and is not applicable to purchases between traders.

excusable mistake or only quite small payments remain to be settled.[5] However where the purchaser has committed a fraud or forgery in respect of the seller the retention of title clause will be maintained so long as the seller has acted expeditiously and in good faith in respect of the goods.[6]

Repossession of the Goods

A pre-condition to the above is that the buyer is in breach of his contractual payment obligation. Section 29 of the Credit Agreements Act further states that the purchaser shall have failed to pay the claimed amount 30 days after due payment, and that the amount must constitute either the entire unpaid balance of 10 per cent of the total amount due, or if several instalments are unpaid, 5 per cent. It should be noted that pursuant to s.37 of the Act, the purchaser can prevent repossession by paying the amount due with interest and costs before repossession has occurred.

It is necessary for the seller to be able to prove with sufficient particularity in which object he has a retention of title. As such, it is prudent for the seller to contain in the sales contract a description of the object so that it can be identified on re-possession.[7] With the assistance of the Bailiff the seller can repossess the object sold without judgment solely

---

5 See *U 1979 740 H.* This case involved the sale of a car for DKK 91,126. The cash down payment was mistakenly stated to be DKK 18,126 which was 19.9 per cent of the purchase price. It was held that the retention of title clause was invalid.

6 See *U 1968 569 Ø.* A car dealer sold a truck subject to a retention of title clause and received from the purchaser as part of the down payment a used truck in exchange and this was guaranteed to be free from encumbrances. This was not the position, even so, the retention of title clause was held valid as the seller when he entered into the agreement did not have any reason to doubt the purchaser and he believed that he was entering into the purchase agreement having received the full amount of the minimum down payment.

7 See *U 1987 629 H.* In this case the seller delivered pigs subject to a retention of title clause to the purchaser who was a farmer. It was agreed in the contract that the pigs should be marked but this was not done even though the seller knew that the farmer had other pigs. As the identification of the pigs in the contract rested solely on the seller's information, the retention of title clause could not be upheld against an unpaid mortgagee who had taken over the property in the pigs and had conducted a foreclosure sale.

on the basis of the purchase contract.[8] However it is a condition of a valid repossession that a copy of the contract containing the retention of title clause signed by the purchaser is handed over to him together with a statement of account. In accordance with s.38 of the Credit Agreements Act the unpaid part of the claim, interest on overdue payments and necessary costs in connection with the repossession of the object can be claimed by the seller although s.39 places upon the latter a duty to disgorge any surplus in favour of the buyer. Where the purchaser is a consumer, s.35 of the Act places a duty on the seller to get satisfaction by repossession of the goods and the seller will usually have no claim against the buyer's assets in respect of any residual amounts.[9] In the case of a non consumer debtor the seller may in addition to repossession levy execution on the seller's other assets in respect of any residual amounts outstanding.[10]

Upon repossession the buyer is entitled to keep accessories paid by him so long as these can be removed without damaging the object.[11] Insofar as it is envisaged that the object is going to be consumed in a manufacturing process or undergo essential change of identity the retention of title provision will not extend to the finished product.

Third party purchasers

By definition a buyer subject to a retention of title clause is normally not allowed to resell the goods which constitute the subject of the clause. Where the buyer has wrongfully resold the goods, in principle, Danish law allows the original seller to repossess the goods from a later buyer. However this will not apply if the seller has been incautious or passive.[12] The Danish principle of *forhandlergrundsaetningen* is relevant here, namely, a seller may not repossess the goods from a later good faith

---

8 S.36 Credit Agreements Act.

9 S.41 Credit Agreements Act.

10 S.51 (3) Credit Agreements Act.

11 It is an implied term in a conditional sale that the buyer keeps the goods in an acceptable condition and in a good state of repair.

12 See *U 1959. 576 Ø*. In this case a shop handed over silver cutlery without checking the customer's identity. The customer paid with a worthless cheque. It was held that the seller was incautious in the sale and could not thereby rely upon a retention of title clause against an innocent third party purchaser (an antique dealer) who had bought the cutlery from the rogue.

purchaser if the seller had handed over the object to a party whom he knew or ought to have known would resell it.

Sale on consignment. The seller may sell goods on a consignment basis indicating that the seller retained title to the object for the time being until resale by the buyer. Typically sales on a consignment basis are not covered by the Credit Agreements Act.[13] Even so, it follows from Danish case law that the same principles which have emerged in respect of retention of title clauses also apply to sales made on a consignment basis. Furthermore, it is required that the seller is paid the outstanding amount of each of the objects concurrently with the resale of each object and that the buyer is under an obligation to keep separate accounts of sales made on a consignment basis whilst the seller is under a duty to other creditors to check the stock of the consignment buyer.[14]

The car registry. Normally there is no registration requirement in respect of chattels under Danish law. However, an exception to this rule is that retention of title clauses in respect of motor vehicles, trailers as well as caravans have to be registered in the Registry of Cars (*bibogen*) if such a clause is to be effective against the buyer's creditors and purchasers. Even so, there is no requirement to register retention of title clauses in respect of vehicles subject to a consignment plan because the registration requirement is restricted to the point of sale from the dealer.

---

13 S.2 (2) Credit Agreements Act.

14 See *U. 1980. 597 SH.* This involved a consignment agreement in respect of stock which was supposed to be checked on the last day of each month and the objects which had been taken out of stock were supposed to be paid within six months. Three years after the agreement was entered into the buyer suspended his payments. The seller sought to recover the goods but on examination it was found that two thirds of the bills were outstanding for a period of up to 10-13 months. It was held that the credit obtained by the buyer in this way was the basis upon which the buyer stayed in business and accordingly the retention of title clause was not upheld in respect of the company's other creditors.

4 Finland

MAGNUS POUSETTE AND SEBASTIAN JÄGERHORN

Introduction

The roots of systematic distinction in Finnish law are mainly to be found in European continental law as represented by German law. Accordingly, under the Finnish civil law one of the main distinctions is between *the law of obligations* and *the law of property*. The law of obligations applies to relationships between contracting parties, that is, *inter partes*. On the other hand, property rights have been deemed to relate to objects and to be protected rights with regard to third parties. The principle of publicity is central in establishing rights under Finnish property law. This principle presupposes that legal effects extending to third parties must be distinctively manifested and the means to achieve publicity are, above all, possession and registration. The purpose of the notice is to protect a third party relying on such indications of legally valid ownership.

The principal rule under Finnish law is that goods sold may not be withdrawn by the seller after the purchaser has taken the physical possession of the goods. Insofar as Finnish law recognises retention of title this is an exception to the general rule. A retention of title clause ("*omistuksenpidätysehto*") is a provision where a seller retains the title to the goods subject to sale until an agreed term - usually concerning payment of the entire purchase price - is fulfilled. Transfer of title is thereby suspended for the purpose of securing the seller against the risk of non-compliance by the purchaser.

The Legal Framework for Retention of Title

There is no specific legislation regarding retention of title clauses in Finland and legal practice is fairly limited. Nevertheless, there are two Acts that concern the use of retention of title provision for certain types of purchase agreements, the Act on Hire Purchase Agreements (18.2.1966/91, as amended) and the Consumer Protection Act (20.1.1978/38). Finnish law defines hire purchase agreements as those for the sale of movable property where the purchase price is paid in (multiple) instalments of which at least one is paid after the transfer of the physical possession of the goods, and where the seller has retained the title to the goods or the right to withdraw the goods until the purchase price has been paid in full. The Hire Purchase Agreement Act is applicable where the substance of the agreement is of a hire purchase character - the heading of the agreement is without relevance. The Act protects the purchaser by way of mandatory provisions which stipulate the consequences of failure to pay the purchase price as agreed.

To balance the protection of the purchaser, the Hire Purchase Agreement Act grants the seller an extraordinary means of enforcing his rights. The seller may, directly and without a court decision, receive executive assistance for repossessing the goods so long as the purchaser has violated his payment obligation to an effect stipulated in the Act. Even where the seller is entitled to withdraw his goods and does so in accordance with the Act, the purchaser is entitled to redeem the goods within 14 days by paying the remaining amount. The redemption period may be up to four months if the delay has been caused by illness, unemployment or other social reasons beyond the purchaser's control (the so-called *social force majeure*). Significantly the Consumer Protection Act contains even further protection for consumer purchasers. Depending on the applicability of the aforementioned legislation, retention of title clauses may be categorised into four groups: first, purchases to which *neither* the Act on Hire Purchase Agreements nor the Consumer Protection Act apply, that is, business to business sales agreements where the purchase price is intended to be paid in one lump sum; second, purchases to which *only* the Act on Hire Purchase Agreements applies, that is, where the purchaser is a business and the purchase price is intended to be paid in multiple instalments; third, purchases to which *both* the Act on Hire Purchase Agreements and the Consumer Protection Act apply, that is, where the purchaser is a consumer and the seller is a business and the purchase price is intended to be paid in multiple instalments; fourth, purchases to which *only* the Consumer Protection Act applies, that is, where the purchaser is a consumer and the seller is a business but the purchase price is intended to be paid in a lump sum.

Retention of title clauses are subject to the consent of both parties and evidentially it is important (but not necessary) that the parties agree to such clauses in writing. There is no requirement as to the form of retention of title clauses save for those in connection with hire purchase agreements. The Act on Hire Purchase Agreements contains a provision according to which hire purchase agreements shall be made in writing by observing a form as specified by legal authority. Should the specified form not be observed, this does not, according to prevailing legal practice, lead to invalidity of retention of title. However, when the specified form is not used, the seller loses his right to claim certain expenses and interest and also the seller loses his special rights to quick enforcement. It should be noted that some retention of title clauses must be registered with the appropriate public authority in order to be valid against creditors of the possessor. This is the case with immovable property and with certain vehicles.

The validity of retention of title clauses

The general prerequisites for a valid retention of title clause are: first, it must be expressly agreed at the latest when the goods are physically transferred to the purchaser;[1] second, the object to which the agreement relates must be identified specifically; third, the purchaser's claim must be based on either the purchase price or on costs attributable to the purchase object. The seller must within a reasonable time assert his rights to reclaim the goods, otherwise the seller risks forfeiting this right.

The validity of retention of title clauses insofar as they impact upon third parties is limited under the so-called rule of non-validity if the initial intention is that the purchaser acquires the goods for resale in the course of his business, or, that he will attach the goods to other property, for example, by way of accession. The rule on non-validity does not presuppose that the third party must be in good faith The Supreme Court has in several cases considered retention of title clauses to be non-valid as against the creditors of a purchaser, even if resale or accession has not yet taken place and even if the goods are in the possession of the purchaser. A retention of title clause does not limit the purchaser's right to resell the

---

1 Retention of title clauses in Finland may not in terms of legal validity be solely based on business practice or custom. A retention of title clause must be explicit and clear. A purchase agreement in which reference is made to general terms of sale which include a retention of title provision is not necessarily binding (see Supreme Court Decision 1993/45). The parties have to agree upon this, at the latest, at the time when the goods are physically transferred to the buyer. According to Finnish legal practice creditors of a buyer have not been deemed bound by retention of title clauses agreed upon after the physical transfer of the goods (Supreme Court Decision 1993/45). Similarly, retention of title clauses have not been regarded as binding against the creditors of the buyer where the clause merely has been printed on the invoice.

goods where the goods were purchased for resale. It is worthwhile noting that scant and not entirely homogenous legal practice indicates that the efficacy of retention or title clauses cannot be determined in advance with full certainty. The specific differences between Supreme Court decisions may affect the effectiveness of retention of title clauses. The Supreme Court decision 1990/104 sets an example of an *exception* to the aforementioned rule of non-validity as concerns goods for resale. In this case, the retention of title clause was effective against a successor purchaser who purchased a whole store of goods (sold for the purpose of being resold) - encumbered by a retention of title clause - from a company which was in the process of winding up. Due to the facts of the case, the successor purchaser was considered to have lacked good faith.

A valid retention of title provision has the effect that the buyer may not resell the goods which are not his property. Clearly, if the purchaser resells the goods in these circumstances this will amount to a breach of contract. In terms of effect on third party purchasers with the exception of situations covered by the rule of non-validity, the retention of title provision will bind successors from the purchaser. This is a consequence of the legal principle according to which successors may not receive a "better right" than that of the assignor except where the subsequent purchaser is in good faith and comes within the principles set out in the Finnish Trade Code, that is, the original seller/owner's title is extinguished.

The concept of good faith is incorporated in the Trade Code 1734, Chapter 11, s.4 and Chapter 12, s.4.[2] Through centuries of legal practice, it has developed into its current form. A purchaser who has acted in good faith may keep goods purchased from a person who had the custody of the goods, unless the rightful owner wishes to redeem them. If a purchaser is considered to be in bad faith, then the purchaser is obligated to return the goods to the rightful owner without compensation. If the purchaser cannot return the goods, then the purchaser shall compensate the rightful owner for the value of the goods. The rule applies to situations where the seller has received custody of the goods by way of loan, deposition, purchase or the like, but not where the custody has been received by stealing or robbery. In those cases good faith will not protect the successor. Furthermore, the rules on good faith protection do not concern situations

---

[2] The Trade Code is in old Swedish and originates from the time when Finland was part of the Swedish kingdom.

where the seller wrongfully has claimed to be a representative agent of the true owner. Objective criteria are used in the evaluation of good faith notably actual knowledge and inferred knowledge. The degree of care required of a purchaser in this respect will vary depending upon the circumstances of the sale but it should be noted that factual possession of a movable object creates a rebuttable presumption of ownership.

Enforcement

Where the buyer in breach of contract fails to perform his obligations under the sale contract the seller can, on the basis of the retention of title clause, require the purchaser to return the goods. Finnish law generally requires the person seeking enforcement to prove his claim in court. Where the Hire Purchase Agreements Act applies, in addition to the seller being entitled to repossess the goods an account is created whereby the remaining value of the goods is credited in favour of the purchaser and against which the debt of the purchaser is debited. The seller is entitled to receive payment for the unpaid purchase price before other creditors. Furthermore under this legislation so long as the formalities have been completed the seller has the right to receive executive assistance in re-collecting the goods.

As against third parties, a valid retention of title clause prohibits the purchaser from reselling the goods. If, however, the purchaser wilfully acts in breach of the purchase agreement the purchaser may be considered to be guilty of embezzlement under the Finnish Criminal Code. Where the purchaser is considered to have committed a criminal act the seller will be entitled to claim for compensation for any loss suffered due to the criminal act.

Implications of bankruptcy. The overriding effect of a valid retention of title clause is that, in the event of a purchaser's bankruptcy the goods subject to retention of title are not included in the bankrupt's estate and the goods may not be pledged against the debts of the purchaser. The owner of the goods receives a *separatist* position in the bankrupt's estate according to which he may repossess the goods and terminate the purchase agreement. The request for returning the goods has to be filed with the bankrupt's estate. The estate is obligated either to pay the unpaid purchase price (irrespective of whether all of it is due) or to return the goods while the seller shall return the paid portion of the purchase price. Alternatively, the seller may file a claim for the unpaid purchase price.[3]

Private international law considerations

The Vienna (UN) Convention for the International Sale of Goods regulates only the relationship between the purchaser and seller. In this respect, Article 4 (b) of the Convention provides that it does not regulate the possible effects of the agreement on the title to the purchased goods and Finland along with the other Nordic countries has made a reservation to this effect. As regards the validity of a retention of title clause, Finnish Private International Law is currently in the process of being amended to be fully in line with the EC Convention on the Law Applicable to Contractual Obligations. The general conflicts of law rule applicable to the property law aspects of retention of title is *lex rei sitae.* Under this rule, the law governing a property right in goods is that of the place where the goods are situated at the time the property right came into existence.

Retention of title clauses are commonly used in commerce in Finland for the sale of movable goods, as well as immovable property.[4] As such, Finnish law embraces a contract incorporating a retention of title clause as an expression of the intent of the parties. Whilst retention of title clauses are not subject to enforceability against third parties in all circumstances, nonetheless, where such an intent is manifested, it is likely that a Finnish court will enforce this intent at least in respect of the *inter partes* dimension of the contractual relationship.

---

3 Where the purchase is governed by the Hire Purchase Agreements Act, the bankruptcy of the buyer does not, as such, constitute a breach of contract which entitles the seller to demand recollection of the goods.

4 Reservation of title case can also be seen in respect of the administration of property in Finland by promoter contractors. Under this scheme the contractor forms a housing corporation which serves as the project developer. The contractor then signs a contract with the housing corporation for the construction of the building which the housing corporation will own. The contractor desires to market shares in the housing corporation as soon as possible. When selling the share the contractor reserves title to them. In addition, the contractor administers the housing corporation during the construction period.

5 France

MARC SAINT-CÈNE

Introduction

A reservation of title clause is a contractual stipulation whereby a vendor defers the transfer of property in goods to the fulfilment of a particular condition, usually the payment of the price. This clause constitutes a guarantee for the vendor who, should the condition not be fulfilled, will remain proprietor of the merchandise, and can claim it back if it has been delivered. In French law, the principle is that, in matters of sale, the transfer of property occurs once the vendor and purchaser have agreed on the subject-matter of the contract and on the price, even though delivery may not have occurred, nor even the price paid. Hence the utility of the reservation of title clause, which enables the transfer of title to be deferred: transfer will only take place on the day when the price is paid. The validity of reservation of title clauses has never been disputed and is based upon Article 1134 of the Civil Code. As such, French law postulates the autonomy of the will of the parties to a contract. The parties can come to free agreement in respect of any legal arrangement as long as they respect the provisions of law which are "imperative", as well as what the Civil Code regards as "moral principles". Thus, it is possible to derogate from the principles of the Civil Code in the case of sale, as these provisions only apply in the absence of any contractual provision to the contrary. However, until the passing of the *Law of 12 mai 1980* on reservation of title clauses, such clauses had uncertain effect in the case of the insolvency of the purchaser.

Under French sale of goods law, the principle of property transfer is *solo consensu.*[1] As stated above, this rule provides that the sale is complete between the parties, and property transferred to the purchaser from the vendor, once agreement has been reached on the subject-matter of the contract, even though the latter has not been delivered, nor the price paid. However, the rule is of "suppletive effect" and is not obligatory, in other words, the parties may agree to derogate from the rule as, for example, through the retention of title mechanism. This enables the creditor to benefit from a position of priority - that of the proprietor. It has

[1] Article 1583, Civil Code.

been confirmed that such a clause is valid and effective, at least when the parties are *in bonis*, that is, when the parties are not insolvent.

Retention of Title Clauses: The Legal Background

It is recognised that the reservation of title clause is valid between the parties and enforceable against third parties when the purchaser is *in bonis*; on the other hand it was not recognised as enforceable against other creditors of the debtor in the case of an insolvency procedure being commenced against the purchaser. The courts set out this principle in two cases[2] where it was held that the vendor could not, as against the debtors of a purchaser who had become bankrupt, benefit from a reservation of title clause so as to be able to exercise his action for recovery. This principle was based on the fact that the merchandise which had been sold and effectively delivered to the purchaser had become one of the elements of his apparent solvency, that is, ostensible ownership. This rigid position was progressively relaxed.[3] Finally, the enforceability of a reservation of title clause in this way was recognised in a *Law of 12 mai 1980*. This law confirmed that a reservation of title clause is enforceable where the purchaser of goods is subject to an insolvency procedure. The law was incorporated into Article 65 of the *Law of 13 juillet 1967* on corporate liquidations which itself was replaced by the *Law of 25 janvier 1985*, which sets out in Article 121 the principles for reservation of title clauses. These dispositions were modified by a *Law of 10 juin 1994*, which was passed to extend and reinforce the effectiveness of reservation of title clauses so as to cover cases where the goods sold have become incorporated into other goods. Even so, there must still be a written memorandum "before" delivery, so as to avoid fraud. The text provides as follows:

> "Where goods are sold subject to a reservation of title clause subordinating the transfer of the property to the full payment of the price, such goods may also be claimed, as long as they remain in kind at the moment the action is commenced. Such a clause, which may form part of a written document dealing with a number of commercial operations between the parties, where

---

2 *Cour de Cassation, Chambre Commerciale, 28 mars et 22 octobre 1934.*

3 The example of German law, which recognised the validity of such a clause even in the case of bankruptcy, encouraged such relaxation.

> the written document is effective, at the latest, when delivery occurs (. . .). A claim in kind may be exercised in the same way against movable property which is incorporated into other movable property, if it can be removed without damaging the goods themselves or the goods into which they are incorporated. This claim in kind may also be exercised over fungibles if the purchaser has goods of the same type and the same quality." [4]

It follows from this that a reservation of title clause in France is enforceable whether the debtor is *in bonis* or subject to an insolvency procedure.

The transfer of risk is subject to the transfer of the property in the goods and is an application of the principle *res perit domino*. According to this principle, when goods have deteriorated, the owner bears the loss. After delivery and before full payment of the price, the reservation of title clause leaves the risk with the vendor, as the latter has not transferred property in the goods. This position was confirmed in the case of *Mecarex*.[5] The lower courts have followed this case, and in their judgments have underlined that the transfer of risk is linked to the transfer of property. However, these cases give a strict interpretation of the vendor's responsibility, by making him liable only for the risk of loss by *cas fortuit* (act of God).[6] The purchaser, on the other hand, is liable where the deterioration of the goods is due to the lack of care or fault.[7] The purchaser is, in effect, under a duty towards the vendor to conserve the goods.

Third party enforceability of reservation of title clauses

Central here is the *Law of 25 janvier 1985* on the administration and judicial liquidation of companies (as modified). The vendor who has included a reservation of title clause and who remains unpaid (in part or in full) will seek to make use of the reservation of title clause to be in a stronger position than the other creditors of the purchaser, who can merely declare their interest in the liquidation procedure. The *Law of 10 juin 1994* operated in this way, and considerably improved the position of vendors

---

4 *Law No 85-98, 25 janvier 1985*, Article 121, al.2,3.

5 *20 novembre 1979, Dalloz Sirey, 1980.*

6 *Cour d'appel de Rennes 8 juillet 1981, Juris Data, no 40535.*

7 *Ibid Cour d'appel de Rennes; Colmar 22 janvier 1982, Hor c. Milhau, Juris Data no. 41282.*

having a retention of title clause where an insolvency procedure has been commenced against their vendor. Thus Article 121, al.3 states that such a vendor may have an action for recovery of movable property even where the latter has been incorporated into other movable property. The legislator did, however, impose the condition that the goods must be removable without damage to the goods themselves or the goods into which they are incorporated. Furthermore, "the claim in kind may also be exercised on fungibles when the purchaser has goods of the same type and the same quality".[8] Finally, Article 122 of the same Law provides that the action for recovery may be exercised against all or part of the price of the goods on condition that these sums have not been paid, nor paid in kind, nor compensated by the current account between the debtor and the purchaser, on the date of the formal commencement of the insolvency procedure.

If the sub-purchaser has not paid, the original vendor can claim from the former the amount due and, if the vendor does not in this way obtain the whole sum due to him, he may seek the rest under the insolvency procedure. On the other hand, if the sub-purchaser has paid, then a chronological distinction needs to be drawn: if the payment was made before the formal commencement of the insolvency procedure, the claim no longer lies, as the sub-purchaser is discharged of all obligations. Where this is not the case, the original vendor must prove that the payment was made by the sub-purchaser to the debtor after the formal commencement of the insolvency procedure. Thus the *Law of 10 janvier 1994* on the insolvency of companies, which altered the *Law of 25 janvier 1985* on the same subject, introduced a right for the vendor who has a reservation of title clause to trace the goods in which he retains the property in the case where his purchaser is subject to an insolvency procedure - which is contrary to the general principles of French law. The rule in French law, in respect of movable property, is that possession is equivalent to title,[9] that is, the person who has possession of goods is considered to be their owner. However, there are exceptions to this principle, in particular the right to trace attached to a reservation of title clause, and this enables the vendor to exercise his rights over the sold goods subject to the retention of title clause, even though these goods are no longer in his possession. Furthermore, as the provisions of the 1994 Law apply to any clause,

8 *Law No.85-98, 25 janvier 1985*, Article 121, al.3.

9 Article 2279, Civil Code.

provided that the conditions set out in that law are respected, the prerogatives conferred on the vendor with a reservation of title clause are extensive.

Types of reservation of title clauses

Simple clauses and extended clauses. Due to the fact that the validity of reservation of title clauses is based on an exercise of the parties' will,[10] there are many different types of clause - of which two stand out in particular. The first is the simple reservation of title clause, which provides that the vendor remains proprietor of the goods until full payment of the price by the purchaser. To be really effective, the contract containing such a clause should prevent the purchaser from reselling or modifying the goods which are subject to the reservation of title clause. A second type of clause has been developed, the extended or expanded reservation of title clause, by which the vendor reserves the property in the goods to himself in the case where the goods are resold or modified. This extended reservation thus provides for a real tracing right and gives the vendor priority.

The influence of the Law of 10 juin 1994. The distinction between simple and extended reservation of title clauses is crucial, as the French statute only permits the third party enforceability of the former type; the extended clauses are not enforceable against creditors. This type of clause, which is more sophisticated, is clearly less efficient for the protection of the vendor's rights. Nonetheless, such clauses produce certain effects when the purchaser is *in bonis*.

Formalities and insolvency procedures

Article 121, al.2 of the *Law of 25 janvier 1985* provides that a reservation of title clause is enforceable in an insolvency procedure, and specifies the conditions relating to the clause itself. These will now be discussed.

In writing. This condition is fundamental: where the clause is not in writing, the action for recovery must be rejected. Other than this there is no special formula imposed by the statutory provision. An examination of the case law on this point shows that there is a good deal of flexibility in

[10] Article 1134, Civil Code.

the way that it is applied. It is not necessary to show that a special agreement has been signed by the parties. Any current commercial document may constitute the written document required by the law. Nor need the written document consist of one single document; it may constitute several documents read together. The requirements of the law have been further eased by the *Law of 10 juin 1994*, which provides that the clause may be contained in a document dealing with a series of commercial operations agreed between the parties. Thus, henceforth, the clause can be general; it may be inserted in a standard form contract which governs the entirety of contractual relations between the parties. It can cover all deliveries which occur, even over a period of several years. The importance of this modification is self-evident - it facilitates the use of reservation of title clauses, and extends their application. Nonetheless, the reservation of title clause must be agreed in writing, at the latest, at the time delivery takes place.

Acceptance of the clause by the purchaser. To reserve title is a derogation from the provision of Article 1583 of the Civil Code - it must therefore be "agreed". For the clause to have this effect, it must result from the common intention of the vendor and purchaser. This requirement is set out in Article 121, al.2 of the *Law of 25 janvier 1985*. As a result, it is for the person who wishes to avail himself of the clause to prove the existence of an agreement.

When a document which governs the entirety of commercial operations between the parties includes a reservation of title clause, the enforceability of the latter cannot be contested. There is no need to show an agreement for each operation. The acceptance of the clause by the purchaser may be implied, so long as the implied acceptance is certain and uncontestable. It is for the first instance court to determine whether this is the case. Previous dealings are an element to be taken into account in determining whether there has been acceptance. However, this element is in itself insufficient to show that the purchaser has accepted the clause. The extent to which the clause was apparent in the commercial documents is also relevant in determining whether or not the debtor has accepted the clause. In order for the purchaser who is executing the contract to be held to have accepted the clause, his attention should have been drawn to the clause by the vendor in the documents which are submitted to him.

It may be that there are conflicting clauses, one in favour of the vendor who is reserving title, the other a clause of the purchaser rejecting any reservation of title clause in the vendor's documents. The *Cour de Cassation*[11] has held that in such cases, the purchaser's exclusion clause takes priority over the reservation of title clause of the supplier. However, a recent law on honesty and equilibrium in commercial relations[12] has broken with this case law. Article 19 of this law (as inserted into Article 121, al.2 of the *Law of 25 janvier 1985*) provides that a reservation of title clause is enforceable against the purchaser and other debtors unless the parties have agreed "in writing to modify or exclude it". This is clearly favourable to the interest of the vendor and extends the application of reservation of title clauses. An agreement between a purchaser and vendor should, therefore, be formalised in writing if the purchaser seeks to refuse the reservation of title clause proposed by the vendor, or which figures in his general conditions of sale.

A formal refusal by the purchaser to accept the clause before delivery is effective, and the judge may not in such a case proceed to examine the circumstances subsequent to the execution of the contract, which do not result in a retraction of this refusal. A refusal which is expressed prior to the reservation of title clause can only be retracted by an express acceptance. A clause by which the purchaser refuses any reservation of title clause is binding on a supplier who knows of it, unless the latter shows that the purchaser retracted his refusal before delivery. An express refusal by the purchaser to accept a clause is effective when brought to the knowledge of the vendor, unless it is subsequently withdrawn. It does not matter that the refusal is not accepted by the vendor. The information given to the vendor enables the latter to withdraw from the sale if a reservation of title clause is essential for him.

Conditions relating to the goods affected by the clause

Before the 1994 Law, the action for recovery applied to "merchandise". In 1994, this is replaced by the much wider notion of "goods". A reservation of title may be made in respect of corporeal goods such as merchandise, equipment and tools, but also the goodwill of a business, patents, trademarks and other incorporeal goods. It may also apply to immovable property. However, in respect of the goodwill of a business, there is a double requirement of registration - that in respect of the sale of the

---

11 *Chambre Commercial, 25 oct. 1994 et 11 juill 1995, Juris Classeur Périodique, éd.E, 11 779.*

12 *Law no.96-588 of 1er juillet 1996*

goodwill of businesses and also that required by Article 85-5 of *Decree no.85-1388 of 27 décembre 1985*. It is the same for immovable property.

Payment of the price by the judicial administrator or the liquidator. It should firstly be noted that in French law, judicial administrators and liquidators are the officers of the law charged with carrying out the administration or liquidation of insolvent companies. Under Article 121, al.4 of the *Law of 25 janvier 1985*, the judicial administrator or liquidator may object to the action for recovery of the vendor who has a reservation of title clause, by paying the price forthwith. The same paragraph provides that no delay in paying the price is possible without the consent of the creditor who is making the claim. By this means, the legislator is favouring the continuance of the activities of the business by avoiding depriving it of indispensable goods. Also, by providing for payment in cash, the legislator is giving the vendor who has a reservation of title clause a privileged position compared to the other creditors who can only participate in the liquidation procedure, and generally have only a faint hope of being paid (and certainly of being paid rapidly!).

Transfer of reservation of title clauses. The benefit of a reservation of title clause can itself be the subject of a transfer to a third party. The *Law of 25 janvier 1985*, like the *Law of 12 mai 1980*, contains a prohibition on the transfer of a reservation of title clause to the benefit of a third party who has paid the vendor the price of the merchandise on behalf of the purchaser. However, the issue gave rise to controversy in both doctrinal debate and in the case law of the courts, a controversy which was brought to an end to two leading cases of the *Cour de Cassation*, which accepted transfer by subrogation of the reserved property.[13] The established position in French law appears to be: first, the vendor who receives from a third party payment of his claim for the price of the merchandise transfers to this third party the benefit of the reservation of title clause; second, the banker holding a bill of exchange drawn by the vendor on his purchaser is subrogated to the rights of the former as against the latter; third, the assignee of the debt of the sale price[14] has the benefit of the reserved property by the assignor-vendor. These solutions represent a new legal technique for financing the purchase of equipment goods and merchandise.

---

[13] *Cour de Cassation, Chambre Commerciale, 15 mars 1988, Bulletin civil IV, no 106, p 74*

[14] *Dailly Law of 2 janvier 1981.*

The right to take action belongs to the owner of the debt of the sale price, the reservation of title being accessory to the price of sale. Nonetheless, a difficulty remains: putting the principle into effect is based on third parties knowing of the existence of the reservation of title, which requires the setting up of a registration system to give notice of such interests, and this has not happened.

Private international law considerations

Despite numerous attempts to introduce uniform laws in respect of sales subject to reservation of title clauses, no common text has been agreed by the European States. This lack of uniformity is to be deplored, and it is therefore necessary to turn to the classical rules of conflict of laws in order to resolve differences which arise between different national laws. There are three traditional conflict rules which concern reservation of title clauses; the law of contract, the law of sale of goods, and the law of insolvency. There are three categories of connection which go with these three areas of conflict rules. Firstly, the contractual connection imposes recourse to the law freely chosen by the parties when they entered into the contract of sale: this is the *lex contractus*. Then there is the real connection, which aims at property and surety law, the *lex rei sitae*, that is the law of the place where the merchandise is situated at the time the action for recovery is exercised. Finally, there is the connection to the law of insolvency, which is used when an action for recovery is exercised whilst insolvency proceedings are continuing against the purchaser. The law which applies is the *lex fori*, the law of the court which is seized, that is, normally the law of the court where the defendant is domiciled, in the circumstances, the purchaser of the goods sold with a reservation of title clause.

Taking into account the fact that the reservation of title clause is contractual in nature, it seems logical to deduce that the law applicable is the law of the contract. However, according to settled case law, "French law alone is applicable to real rights over movable property situated in France".[15] Even so, when an insolvency procedure is commenced, the insolvency law alone is competent to resolve any conflict related to procedure and, in this respect, ensure equality between creditors. It thus

---

15 *Cour de Cessation, Chambre des Requetes, 24 mai 1933, S 1935, I ,253, note Batiffol / Chambre civile, 3 mai 1973, Revue critique de Droit international Prive, 1974, 1000 note Mezger.*

appears that it is the law of insolvency which is inevitably used to resolve the question of the enforceability or non-enforceability of a reservation of title clause when an insolvency procedure has been commenced at the time of an action for recovery. It follows from this that the *lex fori* will be applied in numerous cases, to the detriment of the *lex rei sitae*. Where a French court deals with a reservation of title clause which is in conformity with the national law of a foreign importer the French court will apply the *lex rei sitae*. For example, an "extended" reservation of title clause which is accepted in German law will not be applied in France because of the constraints imposed by the *Law of 12 mai 1980*. Therefore, the reservation of title clause will not have effect and the protection that the vendor thought he had through the clause will prove to be illusory.

Reservation of title clauses have assumed an even greater role in French commercial life particularly following the passage of the *Law of 10 juin 1994*. This law improved the position of a seller of goods on the insolvency of the buyer to such an extent that retention of title has been referred to as the "queen of securities". Because of the absence of harmonisation on the international level, it is for the vendors or purchasers involved in exporting or importing goods to ascertain the applicable law and to abide by the legal requirements of the country concerned. Foreign law is diverse on this issue and it is regrettable in the light of the need to bolster security interests that a uniform approach to reservation of title has not been carried out, especially within the European context as this would simplify the use of these clauses in trade within the European Union .

Translated by Andrew West, Lecturer in Law, University of Wales, Swansea.

6 Germany

BERND WAAS

Introduction

The contract of sale is a mutual contract whereby the seller promises to deliver goods and the purchaser in return promises to pay the purchase price. In practical terms the purchaser is often unable to pay the purchase price to the seller unless he has had the opportunity to sell the goods to his customers or perhaps to incorporate them in a manufacturing process and then sell on the new product to customers which will generate proceeds out of which the buyer will pay the original seller. The purpose of a retention of title clause is to secure the position of the seller where delivery of goods has taken place without payment having been made. If the parties have agreed on retention of ownership according to section 455 of the German Civil Code this contractual stipulation is presumed to mean that the passing of the title in the goods from the seller to the purchaser is subject to a condition precedent, namely, that the purchase price is fully paid by the purchaser. Only if this requirement is met is title transferred from the seller to the buyer. Retention of title is in Germany the most important means of securing the position of a person who delivers goods to another where payment is deferred. In terms of scope, its main area of operation is in the field of sales contracts but is by no means restricted to this type of contract. For instance, a contract for work and materials can contain a retention of title clause too because, though it involves the supply of skill and labour, it also results in a transfer of goods which can be made the subject of a retention of ownership by the parties concerned.

In Germany, the law dealing with retention of title clauses is essentially judge-made law developed by the courts. Only in section 455 of the German Civil Code has the legislator made provision in this regard. Apart from that, standard terms[1] play an eminent role in shaping the law on retention of title clauses. Retention of title clauses are widespread in Germany. As a matter of fact general conditions of business usually provide that ownership in the goods is retained until they are paid for in

---

1 *Allgemeine Geschaftsbedingungen* which are covered by the Act on General Conditions of Business of 1976, *Gesetz zur Regelung des Rechts der Allgemeinen Geschaftsbedingungen* or AGBG.

full. From a practical point of view the major advantage of retention of title clauses lies in the fact that the alternative of pledging movables would be by far more onerous for the parties because according to section 1205 of the Civil Code the pledgor must give up possession of the goods entirely.[2] This would be very tiresome in practice: normally a merchant cannot give up possession of his goods in order to get credit for the simple reason that he needs them either to trade with or them to use them in the process of manufacturing. This is the reason why the pledge mechanism is hardly ever used in order to raise credit, at least not as far as movables are concerned. However, one should not ignore a major drawback of retention of title clauses: the fact that a merchant has huge stocks of goods, practically speaking, is almost irrelevant to the determination of what his true financial position is. It may very well be that all his goods are subject to retention of title clauses and other forms of securities which do not require the giving up of possession. For that reason an unsecured creditor in the case of insolvency may find out to his disadvantage that all goods have been made over to third parties. On the other hand, it would clearly be unjust to take this point too far because, all told, the purchaser gets possession of the goods immediately which is in the general interest of all his creditors, whether they be secured or not.

At the very heart of the law on retention of title in Germany is the differentiation in the German Civil Code (*Bürgerliches Gesetzbuch, BGB*) between the contractual obligation to sell or to buy, respectively and the performance of this duty. The former is nothing more than an act of obligation (*Verpflichtungsgeschaft*), created by the sales contract, under which the purchaser has the duty to transfer the property. The performance of this duty is achieved by, firstly, the physical transfer of possession or its equivalent and, secondly, by a specific consent of the parties concerned to transfer the property. Thus, under German law, two separate agreements have to be distinguished: the contractual agreement which provides the legal basis for the obligation to transfer and the agreement to transfer the property. This dichotomy follows the principle of separation (*Trennungsprinzip*) according to which both transactions are independent of each other. The main consequence is that the nullity of one agreement does not affect the validity of the other agreement.[3] In practical terms, however, the differentiation between the two contracts should not be

---

2 This is the so-called principle of publicity or *Publizitatsprinzip*

3 This is so-called principle of abstraction or *Abstraktionsprinzip*.

overstated for, in the absence of a specific stipulation to the contrary, the consent to the transfer of title can usually be found to be implied in the delivery of goods.

The differentiation between the real transaction by which the contract of sale is performed and the obligation to which the contract gives rise applies equally to the acquisition of ownership in movables as well as to land. Accordingly, the transfer of ownership in land requires an agreement between the parties concerned, whereas delivery which is the second requirement for transfer of ownership in movables is substituted by entry of the interest in a land register, the so-called *Grundbuch.* However, it must be noted in this context that according to section 925 (2) of the Civil Code the agreement between the seller and the purchaser of land is null and void if it is made either under a condition precedent or a condition subsequent. It is for this reason that retention of title is restricted only to the area of the acquisition of ownership in movables.

Retention of Title Clauses: The Legal Background

In stark contrast to other civilian legal systems a reservation of title clause is not subject to a registration requirement under German Law nor are there any other formal requirements. As such, a retention of title clause provides a highly efficient means for securing the payment claims of a seller.

Agreement as to the retention of title as part of the contract of sale

Retention of title by the seller is not the result of a legal rule or a statutory provision but follows from a contractual stipulation between the parties to this effect. If the parties enter into an agreement as to retention of title this is expressed in the contract itself or in the general conditions of business (*Allgemeine Geschäftsbedingungen*). According to the differentiation outlined above two agreements have to be distinguished: as for the level of the so-called *Verpflichtungsgeschäft*, the parties agree that the purchaser will become owner of the goods when he has fully performed his duty to pay. As far as the level of the *Verpflichtungsgeschäft* is concerned it is agreed that ownership is transferred to the purchaser under the condition precedent that the purchase price is fully paid.

Agreement as to the retention of title after the contract of sale has been concluded (nachträglicher Eigentumsvorbehalt)

When the contract is silent as to retention of title opinions are divided in Germany as to whether such a clause can be implied (*ergänzende Vertragslegung*). No such clause can be implied on the basis that it is a custom among merchants to the effect that the seller of goods always retains title until the purchaser has paid the purchase price in full.[4] However, the parties are not prevented from agreeing on a retention of title clause after they have concluded the contract of sale and the contract to transfer the goods.

Agreement as to the retention of title after contract of sale has been concluded but before property is actually delivered. In this circumstance the parties are free to amend their agreement by incorporating a retention of title clause into the contract. Accordingly, the agreement to deliver the property is made to contain a condition precedent to the effect that the purchase price is fully paid. Practically speaking, the seller sometimes tries to influence the purchaser unduly in this regard by declaring, contrary to the original terms of the contract, that he is only willing to transfer the property if the purchaser agrees on the amendment of the contract. In this case, however, there is no obligation for the purchaser to consent. Thus, if the purchaser simply refers the seller to the original agreement, the latter remains under an obligation to transfer the property unconditionally. Only if the purchaser agrees can the original contract be amended and regarded as containing a retention of title clause. If the seller insists on the amendment, but the purchaser is not prepared to amend the original agreement the title does not pass from the former to the latter neither immediately nor later because the parties have not reached an agreement as to the transfer of ownership.[5] However, the seller is still obliged to agree to an unconditional passing of the title under the terms to the original contract of sale and the purchaser, accordingly, may make a claim for specific performance of the original obligation.

Apart from the question of consent it must be stressed that a unilateral declaration of the seller after conclusion of the contract of sale to the effect

---

4 See *RGZ* vol.143, p.14; Collection of the Judgements of the *Reichsgericht*, the predecessor of the Federal Civil Court or *Bundesgerichtshof.*

5 *BGHZ* vol.64, pp.395, 397, Collection of the Federal Civil Court or *Bundesgerichtshof.*

that he wants to retain title can only lead to amendment of the contract if this declaration is sufficiently precise. In particular, it may not be sufficient simply to include a retention of title clause in the fine print of an invoice which is received by the purchaser after the time of delivery of the goods. If, for instance, an invoice contains a declaration as to the retention of ownership (which in itself is unambiguous) the courts will not be prepared to approach the idea of an amendment being made to the original contract of sale if the invoice was received by a junior staff member of the purchaser who cannot be regarded as an agent of the purchaser.

Agreement as to the retention of title after contract of sale has been concluded and after property is actually delivered. Even if the property has been delivered from the seller to the purchaser the parties are free to create the same legal situation as would have existed had they agreed earlier on a retention of title clause. One means of doing so would be for the purchaser to re-transfer the property to the seller who would then transfer to the purchaser the same property subject to the condition precedent that the purchase price is fully paid. In this case a change of the actual possession of the goods is not required because according to section 930 of the German Civil Code property can be transferred even without a change of possession if only the transferee is able to claim so-called indirect or mediate possession.[6] Another means of achieving this would be for the purchaser to re-transfer the property to the seller under the condition subsequent that the purchase price is fully paid.[7] It is a question of interpretation of the contract whether the parties have chosen one way or the other. In any event, consent by the purchaser is crucial.

Conflicting contractual terms. Major problems can arise if both parties to the contract make use of general conditions of business. If the general conditions of business used by the seller contain a retention of title clause whereas the standard terms used by the purchaser contain a provision which prevents the counterpart from introducing a retention of title clause (the so-called defensive clause or *Abwehrklausel*), there is no consent in this respect and, consequently, no retention of title clause is agreed upon.[8] If the seller is not prepared to agree on an unconditional transfer of the title

---

6 Section 868 of the Civil Code.

7 See Federal Civil Court, in *Neue Juristische Wochenschrift* 1953, p.217 with annotation by *Raiser*.

8 See *BGHZ* vol.61, p.282.

the purchaser must bring an action for specific performance in order to become owner of the goods.

Legal effect of retention of title

As far as the contract of sale is concerned a retention of title clause has only little effect. The purchaser remains under an obligation to pay the price for the goods, though he has to fulfil his obligation only if the price is fully paid. As for the transfer of risk[9] and the liability for defects in the things purchased[10] the general rules under the Civil Code will apply. There is one essential modification of the contract of sale if a retention of title clause has been stipulated. This modification concerns the situation where the purchaser is late in payment. In this case, according to section 455 of the German Civil Code, the contract of sale is presumed to contain a stipulation to the effect that the seller is free to rescind the contract. In other words, on the basis of a reservation of title clause the seller enjoys a right to demand an immediate return of the goods if the purchaser is in default of payment. This is an exception to the general rule as laid down in section 326 (1) of the German Civil Code where it is stated that the creditor must fix an adequate extension period for payment (*Nachfrist*) and warn the seller that, if he does not meet his obligation, he will rescind from the contract (*Ablehnungsandrohung*). If the purchaser actually has rescinded the contract, by operation of law each party is obliged to give back what he received under the original contract.[11] Accordingly, if the seller rescinds the purchaser loses both his right of possession and his inchoate ownership (*Anwartschaftsrecht*). The seller, on the other hand, is free to re-claim his property.[12]

It must be noted that sales of movables which are to be paid for by financed instalments are covered by a specific law, the Consumer Credit Act 1991, *Verbraucherkreditgesetz*. If the purchaser is a consumer and credit is used for private and not business purposes special rules apply.

Legal effect of retention of title on the agreement to transfer the property. As far as the agreement to transfer the property is concerned a retention of title clause has the effect that the title only passes to the purchaser if the

---

9 Sections 446, 447 of the Civil Code.

10 Sections 459 ff. of the Civil Code.

11 Sections 346 ff. of the Civil Code.

12 Section 985 of the Civil Code.

purchase price is fully paid by him. This means for instance that the purchaser does not become a partial owner of the goods delivered by making part-payments to the seller. Although he does not become the owner of the goods, so long as the purchase price is not fully paid he is still in possession of the goods delivered and enjoys a right to possess. Accordingly, in terms of possession the seller enjoys no more than indirect possession[13] whereas the purchaser is the (lawful) immediate possessor of the goods.

Legal position of the purchaser. If the parties to a contract of sale have agreed on a retention of title clause the purchaser does not acquire a title until the purchase price is fully paid. However, his legal position with regard to the goods is relatively strong because acquisition of the goods is only dependent on the fulfilment of the condition precedent that he pays the purchase price in full. Apart from that nobody, not even the original owner, can prevent the purchaser from becoming the owner of the goods. Against this background the courts in Germany began to realise that the purchaser deserved legal protection at an earlier stage and recognised the so-called *Anwartschaftsrecht*, or inchoate ownership, thereby protecting the purchaser's expectation of acquiring title.[14] In many respects this is a minor form of ownership. For instance, it can be transferred independently (according to the rules which apply to the transfer of ownership) and even pledged. Like property *Anwartschaftsrecht* is protected against dispossession and other invasions and if the seller is not the owner of the goods the purchaser may acquire *Anwartschaftsrecht* in good faith by analogy to section 932 of the Civil Code which enshrines the principle of acquisition in good faith. This means, in practical terms, that the purchaser who has acquired inchoate ownership as a result of acquisition in good faith becomes owner of the goods even if he knows when paying the purchase price that the seller is not the true owner of the goods.[15] However, it must be stressed that although the *Anwartschaftsrecht* works more or less like ownership, it also depends on the continuing validity of the contract of sale so it would cease if the contract were rescinded.

Termination of reservation of ownership. Normally, reservation of ownership is terminated if the purchase price is fully paid by the purchaser.

---

[13] Section 868 of the Civil Code.

[14] *BGHZ* vol.20, p.88.

[15] *BGHZ* vol.10, pp.69, 70.

Otherwise termination occurs as follows: first, the purchaser can waive his reserved ownership;[16] second, the seller can consent to a transfer of the title by the seller under his authority.[17] Apart from that, the purchaser may lose his title under the general rules of the law of property. According to sections 932 ff. of the Civil Code a purchaser acquires a good title to the goods, provided he buys them in good faith and without notice of any defect or want of title on the part of the seller. By virtue of sections 946 ff. of the Civil Code a person may acquire a good title to the goods as a result of confusion (*Verbindung*) where the seller's goods become an essential part of a new product, or mixture of these goods with other goods where the goods cannot be separated without making an unreasonable effort (*Vermischung und Vermengung*), or where accession of property of the seller to the property of another person (*Verarbeitung*) has taken place. Against this background the seller often tries to make sure that, if he loses his property as a result of the application of sections 946 ff. of the Civil Code, he at least acquires a title in the new product. This can be achieved if the purchaser agrees to a variation of a simple retention of title clause.

Types of Retention of Title Clauses under German Law

There are various types of retention of title clauses under German Law which serve different practical purposes. First there is the simple clause (*einfacher Eigentumsvorbehalt*). This clause provides that the seller remains owner of the goods until the purchase price has been paid in full. Second, the extended retention of title clause (*erweiterter Eigentumsvorbehalt*) where title is reserved by the seller until all sums payable by the purchaser to the seller have been paid irrespective of whether the underlying obligations arise from the same contract or from other contracts concluded between the purchaser and the seller. Third, prolonged retention of title clause (*verlängerter Eigentumsvorbehalt*) where title is reserved against not only the purchaser but also against his customers (sub-purchasers) until the purchase price is fully paid.

[16] The so-called *Verzicht* which according to the Federal Civil Court can be declared unilaterally by the seller; see *BGH*, in *Neue Juristische Wochenschrift* 1958, p.1231.

[17] Section 185 (1) of the Civil Code.

We have already considered the background to simple retention of title clause. In this section we shall examine the extended and more extended clauses.

Extended retention of title clause (erweiterter Eigentumsvorbehalt)

The extended retention of title clause (*erweiterter Eigentumsvorbehalt*) comes in two different sub-types, the so-called "current account" clause (*Kontokorrentvorbehalt*) and the "group of companies" clause (*Kinzernvorbehalt*).

The "current account" clause (Kontokorrentvorbehalt). Very often delivery of goods is not a one time affair but part of a long-standing business relationship. In this case the payment claims of the seller against the purchaser are not normally settled individually for each delivery but rather at regular intervals on the basis of a running account and reservation of title clauses will often provide that the seller retains the ownership in the goods until the account has been fully settled by the purchaser. This type of retention clause has met with some resistance. In particular, it is argued that such a stipulation is unfair because, practically speaking, the purchaser is prevented from becoming owner of the goods as long as the business relationship with the purchaser is not terminated and the purchaser has not paid the purchase price for all goods delivered by the seller. Accordingly, some scholars in Germany regard these clauses as null and void. The courts, on the other hand, do not object to these clauses provided that the parties are merchants. Even so, current account clauses are constructed restrictively by the courts. For example, the Federal Court has held that the title in goods is transferred from the seller to the purchaser, so long as the latter has settled all the claims against him at one point in time, notwithstanding the fact that later on new obligations arise from the business relationship between the two persons.[18] At the same time the Federal Civil Court is also prepared to regard a current account clause as void if in the light of the circumstances of a particular case, the clause is seen as an abuse of the freedom of contract, for example, if the arrangement leads to a situation where the purchaser suffers a gross disadvantage to the benefit of the seller because the value of the collateral unreasonably exceeds the secured debt.[19]

---

18 *BHG, Neue Juristische Wochenschrift* 1978, p.632.

19 *BGHZ* vol.94, pp.105,111.

The "group of companies" clause (Konzernvorbehalt). This is rarely used and is therefore only of minor importance. Under this clause the title in goods is reserved by the owner until the purchaser has met all the outstanding obligations between him and the seller and, in addition to that, all obligations between him and an enterprise which belongs to the same group of companies (*Konzern*) as the seller. The prevailing view is that such a clause is illegal, because in practical terms the purchaser is almost prevented from becoming the owner of the goods and accordingly it is widely regarded as restricting the purchaser unfairly and unreasonably in his economic freedom.

The prolonged retention of title clause (verlängerter Eigentumsvorbehalt)

The prolonged retention of title clause is based on the fact that the seller normally uses the goods delivered either by manufacturing new goods or by selling the goods received by the seller to his customers. By virtue of this clause the seller empowers the purchaser to transfer the property to a third party (*Ermächtigung*). This authority conferred from the owner to the purchaser is necessary because the title has been reserved by the seller, which means that without his consent the *nemo dat quod non habet* rule would apply to a transfer of his property by the purchaser. However, it must be noted that the authority to transfer the property is restricted to occasions where the goods are re-sold in the normal course of business. This, for instance, prevents the purchaser from selling the goods at prices far below the market price or to transfer the property to a company that is on the brink of insolvency.[20] If, on the other hand, the requirements of the authority to sell are met by the purchaser, the seller loses his title and the third party becomes owner of the goods. As a substitute for the loss of his title the purchaser or re-seller in advance cedes his right to claim the purchase price from his customers to the original seller (*Vorausabtretung*).[21] As a result, though the original seller loses his property, he gains the right to sue the customers of the purchaser or re-seller for the purchase price, which means that the underlying rights between the purchaser or re-seller and the third party serve as security for the right of the seller to claim the purchase price from the purchaser.

---

20 *BGHZ* vol.68, pp.199,202.

21 It must be noted that under German Law claims can be assigned by mere agreement; section 398 of the Civil Code.

Validity of assignment of future claims (Vorausabtretung). According to the courts there are no objections against a stipulation under which the purchaser of re-seller cedes his rights against his customers in advance because such a clause does not amount to a serious restriction of his economic freedom.[22] However, there is one requirement which has to be met, namely, that the rights of the purchaser which are the subject of the assignment, can be identified in advance. This means that at the very moment a claim of the purchaser comes into existence, it must be possible to tell whether it is part of the agreement between him and the seller to cede his claims to the latter.[23] In practical terms this requirement often causes problems, particularly where rights are ceded only partly to the seller or where large quantities of goods are delivered on the basis of a continuing business relationship. For this reason retention of title clauses must be drafted with care in order to avoid the possibility that they will be regarded as void by the courts on the ground that the claims due to the specific circumstances in a given case cannot be individualised.

Further, there is the requirement under German Law that it must be legally admissible for the purchaser or re-seller to cede his rights against a third party. This requirement is not fulfilled if the purchaser and his customer have agreed a prohibition stipulation, according to which the former is prevented from ceding his rights against the third party to another person.[24] In this situation, the creditor without the consent of the debtor is not allowed to transfer the right which is the basis for the debt. Where there is no express agreement to the contrary, it is presumed that the seller does not lose his reserved property if the purchaser is legally prevented from ceding his rights, which may arise from a purchase of the goods by a third party. In other words, the authority to transfer the property to another person, normally must be regarded as being limited to the situation where the purchaser or re-seller, is able to deliver a right against his customer as a substitute for the loss of the property of the seller. As a result a prevention of an assignment of rights agreed upon between the purchaser or re-seller on the one hand and a third party on the other hand regularly gives rise to a right of the original seller against the third party to recover the goods.[25] The reason for this is that, though in principle the risk of a transfer by the re-seller to a *bona fide* purchaser cannot be avoided by a retention of title

22 *BGH*, in *Zeitschrift fur Insolvenzpraxis* 1987, pp.85, 87.

23 See for example *BGHZ* vol.79, pp.16, 20.

24 Section 399 of the Civil Code.

25 *BGHZ*, in *Neue Juristische Wochenschrift* 1980, pp.2245, 2246.

clause, under these specific circumstances the latter is not regarded as having bought in good faith and accordingly cannot acquire a good title to the goods.

Another difficulty in this area of the law stems from the fact that an agreement as to an assignment of claims in advance may collide with an agreement with another person to the same effect. In this regard it has to be borne in mind that in Germany rights are often ceded in advance to banks or business agents. In principle, under German Law only the prior cession is valid whereas a later assignment is ineffective (the principle of priority or *Prioritatsgrundsatz*). However, an assignment of future claims must not contravene public policy and must especially not involve a degree of moral wrong, constituting a violation of section 138 of the Civil Code. It is under the heading of moral wrong and by applying section 138 of the Civil Code that the courts have come to reverse the result that would apply by a simple application of the principle of priority. If the purchaser has entered into an agreement with his bank under which he is obliged to assign all his future claims (a global assignment or *Globalzession*) the courts regard such an agreement as null and void insofar as it comprises claims which are normally subject to a prolonged retention of title clause.[26] The rationale is that under these circumstances the banks are seen by the courts as inducing their customer to a misrepresentation of their financial position and, in the process, to a breach of a contract because the seller normally enters into a contract of sale under the impression that the purchaser is still free to assign his future claims and to consent to a prolonged retention of title clause. The upshot of this legal reasoning by the courts is that, albeit the principle of priority normally is in favour of the banks, regularly priority is given to the seller and not to the banks. Accordingly, the principle of priority is not more than a mere starting point and, normally, does not provide the legal basis for the final outcomes of a conflict between a supplier on the one hand and a bank on the other. Because the courts so far have not been prepared to consider the argument that a prolonged retention of title might involve a degree of moral wrong because this stipulation could make it almost impossible for a customer to get credit from a bank, it is argued that as a matter of policy the courts consider supplier credit to be more valuable than bank loans. The banks can avoid this result only if they, at the time of the assignment of future

[26] See for example *BGHZ* vol.30, p.149.

claims, waive their rights insofar as they are the subject of a prolonged retention of title clause (*dingliche Teilverzichtsklausel*).

Because prolonged retention of title clauses normally are based on general conditions of business rather than on individual stipulations, before applying section 138 of the Civil Code, the Act on General Conditions of Business of 1976 has to be taken into account. This Act contains a whole range of specific provisions which invalidate a large number of clauses in general conditions of business that deviate from what is regarded by the legislator as a fair and balanced model of a contract. Apart from these specific provisions, there is a general rule embodied in section 9 of the Act on General Conditions of Business of 1976, which renders void clauses that impose an undue burden upon the other party and by doing this contravene the principle of fair dealing and good faith. It is this provision which is applied by the courts in order to ensure that no party can obtain security to an extent which does not correspond to the value of its claims. Accordingly, a stipulation as to the assignment of future claims is null and void if the value of these claims exceeds the value of the claims it is earmarked to secure by the margin of 20 per cent.[27] In this case nullity can only be avoided by stipulating that the purchaser has the right to ask for a waiver of these claims (a release clause or *Freigabeklausel*). Thus, every retention of title clause should contain a provision to the effect that where the value of the sureties accruing to the supplier exceeds the value of all privileged claims by more than 20 per cent, the supplier upon request shall release a respective part of the sureties.

The authority to collect outstanding debt (Einziehungsermächtigung). Normally, an assignment of future claims is accompanied by an agreement under which, with regard to the claims assigned, the purchaser is allowed to act as an agent for the purchaser as far as the collection of outstanding debt is concerned. This means that, though the seller and not the purchaser is the owner of the right, it is the latter who is enabled to claim payment from his customer. It is self-evident that pursuant to the agreement between the parties to the contract of sale the purchaser is obliged to forward the money to the seller immediately. As a rule the third party is not aware of the fact that the seller (who, in terms of the original contract of sale, is the purchaser) does not own the claim for the purchase price, that is, there is a "silent assignment" (*stille Zession*).

---

[27] *BGHZ* vol.120, 300, 304 and *BGHZ* vol.94, 105, 113.

The aggregation clause (Verarbeitungklausel). Where the goods delivered by the seller are used by the purchaser to manufacture other products, section 950 of the Civil Code states that ownership of a new product belongs to the manufacturer provided that the value added to the original goods is not far below the value of these goods. It follows from this that the seller could habitually lose his property when delivering goods to a person whose line of business is manufacturing. However, the operation of section 950 of the Civil Code can be excluded by way of an agreement between the seller and the purchaser under which the latter in his capacity as manufacturer acts as an agent for the seller thus making the former the manufacturer in the sense of section 950 of the Civil Code, and therefore the owner of the goods.[28] As a result, the owner of the original goods, by operation of law, becomes the owner of the new product of which the original goods form a part. In this case the title of the seller in the new product exists under a condition subsequent that the purchase price is paid in full: the manufacturer acquires the title to the new product the very moment he meets his contractual obligation to pay for the goods delivered by the seller.

The problem with this type of clause is that it may favour the seller unfairly because the value of the new product may grossly exceed the value of the original goods. This is especially true where the new product consists not only of the original goods but of goods delivered by other suppliers as well. In this case the underlying clause may be regarded as being in breach of good morals and therefore null and void. In order to prevent this eventuality the parties mostly agree on a contractual stipulation according to which the seller becomes a co-owner of the new product, that is, the seller becomes the owner of the new product only insofar as it does not contain the value of goods which were delivered from other persons. In practice, the courts are only prepared to accept a stipulation to this effect if it is sufficiently precise which means that it must be possible for them to decide upon the question to what extent has the seller become the owner of the new product.[29]

The common German practice is that the parties combine an aggregation with a prolonged retention of title clause. This means that the seller confers an authority on the purchaser to sell the new product ceding his claims to the purchase price against third parties in advance to the

---

[28] See for example *BGHZ* vol.79, p.16.

[29] *BGHZ* vol.46, 117, 122.

original seller. As a result ownership or partial ownership of the new product is transferred to the third party whereas the purchaser or re-seller only becomes owner of the right to the purchase price insofar as he was owner of the product manufactured by him.

A chain of retention of title clauses linking the seller to the purchaser and to a sub-purchaser (weitergeleiteter Eigentumsvorbehalt)

According to this type of retention of title the seller remains owner of the property even if the goods are sold from the purchaser to a third party. However, the purchaser is obliged to inform his customer about his lack of title and accordingly it is agreed between the purchaser and the third party that the title is not passed to the latter until the claim to the purchase price which arises from the original contract is fully paid by the purchaser. This arrangement does not normally fit with the commercial needs of the parties concerned and, for this reason, it is only of marginal importance.

Retention of title passed on to the sub-purchaser (nachgeschalteter Eigentumsvorbehalt)

According to the type of clause the purchaser who is bound by retention of title clause introduces a similar clause into the contract of sale with his customer. If the latter pays the purchase price in full the title immediately is passed to him. It is passed to him from the original buyer where he has become the owner of the goods by fulfilling his obligations toward the seller. Alternatively, it is passed to the sub-buyer by the original seller if he has conferred the authority to transfer the title to the purchaser where the third party fully pays the purchase price.[30]

Retention of title in execution procedures (Zwangsvollstreckung)

If a person is in a position to enforce a court judgment against the purchaser a clerk of the court will seize the goods of the purchaser and, if necessary, sell them in order to pay the plaintiff. As far as goods are concerned which have been made subject to a retention of title clause the seller can prevent a seizure of the goods for the simple reason that he and not the defendant is still their owner. In this case, however, the buyer may

---

[30] *BGHZ* vol.56, 34, 35.

decide to terminate the reservation of ownership by paying the purchase price or the missing part of it to the seller.

Retention of title and the insolvency of the purchaser (Konkurs). Where the purchaser has become insolvent and a receiver (*Konkursverwalter*) is appointed by the court, the receiver has to make a choice as regards the contract of sale and the transfer of property.[31] If the receiver chooses to honour the contractual promise made by the purchaser the purchase price must be paid and the title to the goods will be passed. If the receiver, on the other hand, rescinds the contract the seller can both claim that the goods must be returned to him (*Aussonderung*)[32] and bring an action for damages for breach of contract.

In the case of an extended or a prolonged retention of title the legal situation is more complicated. As for extended retention of title it may happen that the purchaser before opening of bankruptcy proceedings has fully paid for the goods whereas he still has to fulfil other claims which are subject to the retention of title clause. In this case the seller is prevented from simply demanding the return of the goods (*Aussonderungsrecht*) but is restricted to a so-called *Absonderungsrecht.*[33] This means that the seller, though still being the owner of the goods, is treated like a creditor who acquired a lien prior to the opening of the bankruptcy proceedings. As for prolonged retention of title the situation is more or less the same. If the purchaser has already sold the goods and assigned the corresponding claim the seller can only demand separate satisfaction thereof (*Absonderungsrecht*).

Retention of title and conflict of laws

Contracts of sale of goods which cross national borders pose difficult legal problems because the requirements as well as the legal effects of retention of title clauses are governed by international private law. The major problems which arise in this context are due to the fact that the rules which apply to the acquisition of ownership are completely different in the various national legal systems and the same is true so far as the recognition of non-possessory security interests is concerned.

31 Section 17 of the Insolvency Act (*Konkursordnung*).
32 Section 43 of the Insolvency Act.
33 Section 48 of the Insolvency Act.

As for the recognition of foreign securities the *lex rei sitae* applies. Thus, classification is left to the law of the *situs*. Property *in transitu* (movables sold and sent abroad) is governed by the law of the country from which the goods are sent until they are received by the purchaser. According to the prevailing legal opinion in Germany, the law of the country of destination has to be applied as soon as the goods have left the country of origin. Since many foreign legal systems recognise security interests only if certain formal requirements are met and do not recognise a security interest if physical possession is not handed over to the lender the German *Eigentumsvorbehalt* is not recognised in a number of foreign countries.

7 Greece

COSTAS VAINANIDIS

Introduction

Under Greek law the seller is obliged to transfer to the buyer the ownership of the goods sold which involves the transfer of possession with the intention that the latter becomes the owner of the goods, that is, acquisitive prescription. Article 532 of the Greek Civil Code provides that the seller can retain ownership in the goods even though possession has passed and further the buyer shall bear the risk as from the time of delivery. Such a clause retaining title is justified on the basis of freedom of contract: the contracting parties are merely agreeing on how the buyer will perform his obligations and when he will pay the agreed price. In the absence of a specific statutory provision it is not necessary for a retention of title clause to be in writing.[1] Retention of title is normally agreed by the parties upon the conclusion of the sale. It may also be agreed after the conclusion of the sale so long as delivery has not taken place.

It is important to set retention of title clauses within the framework of Greek Contract Law. When the buyer is in default of payment, the seller has the following *alternative* course of action available. First he can claim payment which presupposes that the seller did not rescind the contract of sale and that this is still valid. The seller may claim payment of one or more instalments which are due, whilst those which are not overdue can be claimed either by virtue of Article 386 of the Civil Code, or on the basis of a clause commonly inserted in contracts of sale which provide for automatic acceleration of payments on default. The seller may also claim interest on the deferred payments in accordance with Article 345 of the Civil Code and also any losses he can prove. If the seller chooses to rescind the contract, that is, to bring the contract to an end he simultaneously loses his right to claim payment of the purchase price and the parties must be returned to the *status quo ante*.[2] The seller is entitled to

---

1 For example, the sale of real property must be executed in writing before a notary public. A guarantee must also be in writing. There are formal requirements in respect of the sale of cars which require the intervention of a notary.

2 Article 389 Civil Code.

claim repossession of the item sold and in order to prevent unjust enrichment which is outlawed by virtue of Article 904 of the Civil Code the buyer can recover the price paid. However, the seller may offset the damages awarded to him under Article 383 for non-fulfilment of the contract with the sums which should be disgorged to the buyer on the basis of Article 904. It should be noted that the right of the seller to rescind[3] a sale of goods contract can by virtue of Article 281 of the Civil Code be restricted on the basis of good faith or alternatively, on the basis that, to allow this remedy would be an abuse of right, for example, where the amount overdue is trivial. A further remedy for the seller on default is to claim damages pursuant to Article 383 of the Civil Code for the non fulfilment of the obligations of the buyer. A liquidated damages clause will be upheld to the extent that instalments already paid to the seller can be retained by him as a fair consideration for the use and exploitation of the thing by the buyer during the period before rescission.

The Scope of Retention of Title

Article 532 of the Civil Code presupposes that the retention of title clause applies to tangible assets although by analogy it may also apply to intangible assets. In practice, Article 532 applies predominantly to the sale of movable goods or fixed assets of considerable value, where the purchase price is substantial and it is customary to be paid in instalments. In respect of consumable goods, the seller maintains the ownership under Greek law for so long as the respective goods have not been consumed. A retention of title clause may be applied to the sale of a group of objects or a group of assets under Article 532 so long as each object or asset can be specifically identified and the retention of title will apply separately to each object. Risk passes to the buyer on delivery.[4] In case of damage or destruction of the object delivered due to an unlawful act of a third party the buyer bears the risk and must indemnify the seller, the justification being that the financial value of the object has been transferred to him and he can earn the profit from the exploitation of the goods following delivery. This is

[3] No form is necessary for the exercise of the right of rescission. A mere declaration, even a verbal one addressed to the other party is sufficient.

[4] Article 532 Civil Code. The word "delivery" means the physical delivery, that is, the transfer of possession.

also the case if the goods are destroyed and this is specifically provided for in Article 522 of the Civil Code.[5]

A retention of title clause protects the seller against the claim of third parties such as the creditors of the buyer and also any third party purchasers who are in bad faith. In cases where the buyer purchases goods for resale, retention of title clauses are of doubtful validity since the consent of the seller to the sub-sale will be assumed and the buyer will be deemed to be in good faith. In respect of the sale of movables as a result of an enforced sale by auction, the original seller may under Greek law invoke his ownership to reclaim the goods even after the auction. In the case of the sale of land a retention of title clause will be registered at the land registry and if this is done any third party purchaser or creditor will be deemed to have notice of the clause and, thereby, will not be able to claim that the purchase is in good faith.

Retention of title and insolvency

Two issues are of critical importance in respect of the applicability and enforceability of a clause reserving title to the seller of the goods upon the buyers' bankruptcy, namely, the bankruptcy date and the location of the goods. The seller may enforce a retention of title clause against a bankrupt in the event that the default of the buyer occurred prior to the bankruptcy date and the seller rescinded explicitly or tacitly the contract of sale by claiming repossession of the goods[6] either prior to or after the bankruptcy date. So long as the item is a tangible asset which has not been processed or changed and can be specifically identified the seller can successfully reclaim the asset. The seller's right to rescission however is restricted if the bankrupt was not in default of payment on the bankruptcy date.

Conclusion

Ownership in the property will pass upon payment of the price and this will occur as a matter of law irrespective of the provisions of the retention of title clause. In the case of transactions subject to a written form property will only pass upon completion of the necessary procedural requirements.

---

5 The Penal Code provision may also be relevant in this context.

6 Supreme Court 22/1987 (in Plenary Session); Supreme Court 1381/88; Supreme Court 1039/91; Athens Court of Appeal 816/93.

For example, the transfer of full ownership of real property does not take place prior to the registration with the competent Land Registry of the notarial deed confirming that full payment of the purchase price has been effected.

Retention of title facilitates transactions by offering in the course of day to day business the opportunity for buyers to obtain the immediate use and exploitation of the subject-matter of the sale without paying the full agreed price at the conclusion of the contract. The necessity for formalities under Greek law for retention of title clauses are minimal and this contrasts with other sorts of security such as mortgages and pledges which are normally more costly and complicated to establish for the contracting parties.

8 Italy

ALVISE DONÀ DALLE ROSE

Introduction

The retention of title clause is a contractual mechanism by which the supplier of goods can protect himself against the risk of the insolvency of his customer, by virtue of the power stipulated to repossess the goods delivered. Analytically the sale of goods subject to retention of title postpones the transfer of ownership after delivery (the risk having passed to the buyer at that time) until payment has been made of agreed sums to the seller. In Italy the sale of goods subject to retention of title has developed particularly in the context of "registered movables", for example, cars whereby the seller's interest must be registered and, if so, will prevail against third parties.

The general position as set out in Article 1523 of the Italian Civil Code is that in the case of instalment sales in which ownership in the goods is retained by the vendor, the buyer acquires ownership of the thing upon payment of the last instalment of the price but risk passes at the time of delivery. However, retention of title is not implied by law into sale contracts and, as such, this clause must be expressly incorporated into the agreement. The main characteristic of such a clause is that the risk and other burdens such as maintenance, repair costs and fiscal obligations pass to the purchaser, while the title remains with the seller. During this period the buyer cannot destroy, transform or damage the goods supplied as he has no title in them. Where a third party causes damage to the object subject to the retention of title clause, the seller has the power to sue the buyer for damages to the extent of the outstanding sum owed while the buyer can sue the third party directly for the damage caused. The seller can only sue the third party directly upon termination of the sale contract.

The Basis and Scope of Retention of Title

Third party interests

By virtue of Article 1524 of the Italian Civil Code a reservation of title clause can only be relied upon against the creditors of the buyer if it appears in a written document bearing "a certain date prior to the date of attachment." Further, Article 1524 states that in case of machinery[1] where the price exceeds 30,000 lire, the retention of title clause will prevail against third party interests including a buyer provided that it was registered in a special register kept in the office of the Clerk of the Court having jurisdiction over the place where the machinery is located and so long as when the machinery was acquired by the third person, it was still in the same place where the registration was made. As far as newly manufactured goods and machine tools with a price of at least 500,000 lire are concerned, the so-called *Legge Sabatini* [2] provides that the machine must bear a plate in a prominent position with the name of the seller as owner and information identifying the machine if a reservation of title clause is to prevail against a third party acquirer and this is additional to the requirement of appropriate registration.

The effect of bankruptcy

The retention of title mechanism can only be relied upon in the bankruptcy of the buyer if it is in writing and has a certified date prior to the bankruptcy order. In order to have a certified date the agreement must be registered. The developed position in Italy is that so long as the retention of title agreement is part of the original contract of sale it is not necessarily prejudicial if the registration of the agreement takes place subsequent to entering into it. If he wishes to avoid the retention of title clause, the receiver under Italian law has the burden of proving that the provision was not originally part of the sale contract.

---

1 The general position is governed by Article 1153 of the Italian Civil Code which protects the position of the *bona fide* purchaser and possessor of goods sold by the original buyer.

2 *Law 18 November 1965, No 1329.*

The effect of bankruptcy upon the sale contract is that it does not generally terminate the agreement. Under s.73 of the Bankruptcy Act[3] in this situation the receiver can adopt the buyer's contract with the consent of the Court but on this eventuality the seller is entitled to receive a bond in respect of the price (unless this payment has been made) subject to an appropriate discount for early payment. In the case of an executory sale or partly executed sale, s.72 of the Bankruptcy Act gives the option to the receiver either to adopt the agreement or to terminate it whilst the seller under this provision can by giving him eight days notice place the receiver in default, so that, as soon as the time has elapsed, the agreement will be automatically terminated. Where this occurs the receiver is not considered to be entitled to revoke the payments already made to the seller as instalments of the price.

Termination of the contract

The seller's creditors are not entitled to attach the goods sold under a retention of title clause and obtain a windfall at the expense of the buyer's creditors. Article 1525 of the Italian Civil Code provides that notwithstanding any agreement to the contrary, default of payment of only one instalment which does not exceed one-eighth of the total price does not terminate the contract. Even where the contract is terminated due to the buyer's non-performance, Article 1526 provides that the seller must return the instalments he has received, subject to the right to fair compensation for use of the thing and for damages. This will take into account the natural wear and tear of the goods and the time elapsed. If the agreement provides for a certain sum to be returned by way of an indemnity this can be scrutinised by the court and the judge, according to the circumstances, can grant a reduction of the agreed indemnity.

It is significant that Article 1526 extends to lease contracts although a distinction is drawn between finance leases where ownership is not transferred at the end of the term and a contract in the form of a lease where ownership will pass to the lessee at the end of the term. In the case of the former where termination of the contract occurs due to the buyer's non performance, the leasing company is not under an obligation to reimburse the amount of money already cashed[4] and a clause which provides for the payment of all outstanding rentals at the date of

---

3 *R.D. 16 March 1942, No.267.*

4 An analogy is often drawn here with s.72 of the Bankruptcy Act. See above.

termination is valid. In contrast, where the nature of the contract is by way of hire purchase, an analogy is drawn with a sale agreement subject to a retention of title clause and s.73 of the Bankruptcy Act applies. Thus, in the case of termination of the agreement due to the bankruptcy of the buyer, the leasing company has to reimburse payments already cashed, setting off its credit for fair compensation under Article 1526 of the Civil Code for use of the asset and for damages.

9 Netherlands

GERARD CARRIERE

Introduction

In both national and international transactions involving the sale of goods, title is often retained by the seller until the buyer has fulfilled certain obligations, in most cases, payment of the purchase price. It is quite common for the general sales conditions of suppliers of goods in the Netherlands to contain such a retention of title clause. Retention of title is a security device: the supplier, in effect, obtains security for extending credit to the buyer. Insofar as the goods themselves are concerned, a retention of title represents the most far-reaching type of security which the supplier can have. If the purchase price is not paid, he may reclaim the goods as their unconditional owner, provided the buyer still has them in his possession and they can still be identified. Another advantage of title retention is that it requires no special formalities other than an agreement, which may in principle even be oral; in practice, it is usually provided for in a clause in the supplier's general conditions of supply.

Retention of title clauses are subject to a number of limitations under Dutch law. For example, a retention of title clause cannot be used to give the supplier an interest in the proceeds from the sale of the goods by the buyer to sub-buyers, or in the receivables of the buyer arising from the sale of the goods to sub-buyers. However, since many businesses in the Netherlands are financed by bank loans secured by a (non-possessory and undisclosed) pledge on the borrower's present and future assets, a pledge taken by the supplier under these circumstances will usually rank behind that of the bank. Thus, despite its limitations, a retention of title clause still, in most cases, offers the supplier more effective protection in the event of the buyer's insolvency than the other security devices available to him.

The discussion below will be limited to retention of title in contracts for the sale of goods (other than registered vessels and aircraft) between commercial parties, although title may also be retained in connection with other types of transactions under Dutch law.

Retention of Title Clauses: The Legal Background

Although there are various provisions of the Civil Code which are relevant to title retention, Article 3:92[1] is the only provision specifically devoted to this device. Article 3:92 (1) reads as follows:

> If the purpose of an agreement is to reserve to one party the ownership of property which is placed under the control of the other party until such other party has rendered the performance due, the first party is presumed to undertake to transfer the property to the other party subject to the condition precedent that such performance is rendered.

From the contractual point of view, retention of title is simply a clause in a contract for the sale of goods pursuant to which the parties agree that the supplier will place the goods under the buyer's control, and that the supplier will remain the owner until the full purchase price is paid or certain other obligations are fulfilled.

With respect to the transfer of ownership rights in the goods, (the property law aspect of the transaction), retention of title is characterised under Dutch law as a form of conditional transfer. Both the supplier who retains title to goods sold and the buyer of such goods have a conditional ownership interest. The supplier is the owner subject to a condition subsequent that the buyer fulfils certain obligations: the buyer is the owner subject to a condition precedent that such obligations are fulfilled. The fulfilment of those obligations results in the supplier losing his (conditional) ownership rights and the buyer becoming the unconditional owner by operation of law, without any further legal act being required. A retained title is neither a dependent nor an accessory right, since it is not regarded as being so closely related to the supplier's claim that it cannot exist on its own. This means that a third party to whom the supplier assigns his claim against the buyer does not automatically acquire the supplier's retained title rights. A separate transfer of these rights is required. Since Article 3:92 refers to a *presumption* that the parties agree to transfer the property subject to a condition precedent, the parties may prove that something else has been agreed. For example, they may have agreed that title does not pass automatically upon the fulfilment of the condition, but that a separate deed of transfer is required.

---

1 Unless otherwise indicated, all references in this Chapter to Code Sections are to the Netherlands Civil Code.

Prior to the introduction of the new Civil Code in 1992, there were no statutory provisions dealing specifically with retention of title, and there were no restrictions on the obligations which a retention of title could secure. It was therefore possible for the seller to retain title until the buyer had fulfilled all his obligations to the seller, on whatever legal basis such obligations arose, including, for example, the payment of damages in tort. However, Article 3:92 (2) of the present Civil Code which, like the rest of the new Civil Code, came into effect on 1 January 1992, sets out an exhaustive list of the types of claims which may be secured by a retention of title. These are claims:

(i) regarding the performance due (to the supplier) in exchange for goods supplied or to be supplied (by the supplier to the buyer) pursuant to contract. The performance in question is almost always payment of the purchase price. In the case of a single transaction, title is retained for the payment of the purchase price for the goods supplied in that transaction. It is also possible, however, in the case of ongoing sales, such as by a principal to a distributor, for title to be retained to secure payment for goods supplied in the past and to be supplied in the future;[2]

(ii) regarding the performance due (to the supplier) in exchange for service or activities rendered (by the supplier to the buyer), such as maintenance or service obligations, pursuant to contracts as referred to in (i). For example, if a builder supplies building materials in addition to performing labour, title to the building materials may be retained to secure payment for the building materials as well as the labour;

(iii) for damages arising from a breach by the buyer in performing his obligations under the contracts referred to under (i) and (ii) above. For this purpose, damages includes interest and costs as well as damages payable pursuant to a liquidated damages clause.

---

2 Although there is no definitive case law on this issue, the leading legal authorities interpret the legislative history of Article 3:92 as supporting this view.

A retention of title clause whose purpose is to secure claims other than those set forth above is generally assumed to violate Article 3:84(3) (the so-called prohibition against fiduciary transfers of title) and is therefore null and void. Article 3:84(3) invalidates a purported transfer of title whose purpose is in fact to provide security. However, recent case law of the Netherlands Supreme Court casts some doubt on the (unrestricted) scope of this prohibition.

If the supplier wishes to obtain security for claims other than those enumerated above, he may, in addition to retaining title as security for the enumerated claims, obtain from the buyer a (non-possessory) pledge on the goods as security for such other claims. The creation of such a pledge requires a notorial deed or registered private instrument. If the pledge is granted (in advance) by the buyer prior to the buyer's title becoming unconditional, it will rank above a (non-possessory) pledge (on future assets) which the buyer may already have given to his bank as security for the credit provided. This type of pledge is referred to as a "retained pledge" on the theory that when the buyer acquires absolute ownership of the goods, they are already encumbered. In contrast, if the pledge is given by the buyer to the supplier after the buyer has acquired unconditional title to the goods, the supplier's pledge will rank behind that of a bank as referred to above. Article 3:92 (3) lists a number of events which are regarded as equivalent to performance by the buyer, and which therefore result in the condition precedent being fulfilled and title passing to the buyer. These events are: first, satisfaction of the claim other than by the performance due having been rendered; second, the buyer being discharged from his obligation (pursuant to a court order) on the ground of a default by the supplier; third, the supplier waiving his right to performance by the buyer; and fourthly, the supplier's claim becoming time-barred.

Enforcement

Retention of title to manufactured or processed goods

If the goods sold subject to a retention of title consist of component parts, raw materials, or other goods which will be processed, manufactured, or otherwise used to form new goods, the question which arises is whether the supplier's retained title extends to the newly formed goods. Dutch law does not recognise the extension of retention of title to new goods from which the original goods are formed. As a general rule, a retained title lapses by virtue of accession, *confusio* or *specificatio*. This means that the supplier loses his (conditional) ownership rights in the goods, and the buyer acquires absolute title thereto. However, pursuant to the statutory rules governing accession, *confusio* and *specificatio*, the supplier may, depending on the factual circumstances, acquire (unconditional) co-ownership rights in the goods with the buyer.[3]

Retention of title against subsequent buyers

Under Dutch law, it is not possible to reserve title against sub-buyers of the buyer. Likewise, a retention of title does not and cannot be made to extend to the proceeds of sale arising from sales by the buyer to sub-buyers or to the buyer's receivables arising from such sales. It is possible for the supplier to obtain a pledge from the buyer of his bank accounts or (future) receivables, but this will rank behind a pledge on these assets given previously by the buyer to his bank.

The effect of retention of title clauses

Should the buyer fail to render the performance due, the supplier may demand that the goods be returned and, if necessary, may proceed to seize the goods by a special form of attachment.[4] The buyer must be in default.[5] A notice of default is often required,[6] but not always, in particular not when a period during which performance is due lapses without the obligation being fulfilled.[7] It is generally assumed in the legal literature that the invoking of a retained title automatically entails the rescission of the sales contract. Rescission does not have retrospective effect,[8] but merely creates an obligation to "undo the performance which has already been rendered",[9] in other words to return what has been received or, if that is not possible, to pay compensation therefor. In practice, this generally

---

[3] See below.

[4] *Beslag tot afgifte*: Article 730 Code of Civil Procedure.

[5] Article 6:265 (2).

[6] Article 6:82.

[7] Article 6:83 (a).

[8] Article 6:269.

[9] Article 6:271.

means that the supplier will be obliged to reimburse the buyers for any part of the purchase price already paid.

Conflicts involving rights of third parties. As stated above, both a supplier who has retained title to goods sold and the buyer of such goods have a conditional ownership interest in the goods, the supplier's interest being subject to a condition subsequent and the buyer's being subject to a condition precedent. As long as the condition has not been fulfilled, the supplier has the power to transfer the goods to a third party, but the interest acquired by such third party remains, as a general rule, subject to the condition being fulfilled.[10] Conversely, if the buyer transfers his ownership interest in the goods to a third party, the interest acquired by the third party remains, as a general rule, subject to the condition precedent. The rule that a conditional owner can only transfer a conditional interest is set forth in Article 84(4) and is based on the requirement set forth in Article 84(1) that in order to effect a valid transfer, the transferor must have the power to dispose of the interest which he purports to transfer.

In the case of a transfer by the buyer, some legal writers have argued that where the supplier is aware that the goods are acquired by the buyer for resale, the buyer is impliedly authorised to transfer unconditional title to them to third parties. However, the Supreme Court rejected this argument in 1993, holding that whether the buyer has this authority must be answered by interpreting the agreement creating the retention of title.[11] The mere fact that the goods are intended for resale is not sufficient. Clauses expressly authorising the buyer to resell the goods in the ordinary course of business are quite common. Such a clause would entitle the buyer to sell the goods to his customers, but, as a general rule, would not authorise him to grant a security interest in the goods to his bank.

In some cases it may be possible for a third party who has purchased the goods from the supplier or buyer to obtain unconditional title thereto, despite the supplier's or buyer's conditional ownership rights, based upon Article 3:86. This provides for the protection of certain good faith purchasers for value in the event that the transferor lacks the power to dispose of the interest which he purported to transfer. However, Article 3:86 will generally be of greater use to a subsequent purchaser from the buyer than a subsequent purchaser from the supplier. This is because the

---

10 *Van Essen/NMB*, Netherlands Supreme Court, 28 April 1989, NJ 1990, 252.

11 *Hinck* v *van der Werff* (Netherlands Supreme Court, 14 December 1992, NJ 1993, 623).

buyer will almost always have possession of the goods and a third party will not generally be entitled to believe, in good faith, that the supplier had the power to transfer unconditional title under those circumstances. Only in the unusual situation that the supplier has the goods in his possession, such as for repair, may the third party in come cases be able to claim protection. On the other hand, a third party who has purchased the goods for value from the buyer will often be able to rely on Article 3:86 on the grounds that he neither knew nor should have known about the supplier's interest. Similarly, a third party to whom the buyer has granted a possessory pledge may acquire a valid pledge provided that he was in good faith at the time of the pledge.

Lapse of the retained title. The supplier's (conditional) ownership rights are extinguished in the event that:

(i) the condition precedent, that is, payment of the purchase price and, in some cases, the performance of certain other (collateral) obligations as referred to in Article 3:92 (2) is fulfilled;

(ii) any of the equivalent events enumerated in Article 3:92 (3) occurs, that is, the buyer is discharged from his obligations on the ground of a breach by the supplier,[12] the supplier's claim against the buyer becomes time-barred, and, in the absence of a clause to the contrary, the supplier waives his right to the performance due;[13]

(iii) the buyer transfers the goods to a third party pursuant to an express or implied clause granting him the authority to do so;

(iv) the buyer transfers the goods to a third party without the power to do so, but the third party is a good faith purchaser for value and is entitled to rely upon the statutory provisions protecting third parties;

(v) the goods became part of other goods (or immovables) by accession,[14] and such other goods (or immovables) are to be regarded as the principal goods. If the goods are combined with

[12] Article 6:60.
[13] Article 6:160.
[14] Article 5:14.

other goods in such a way that neither may be regarded as the principal goods, the retention of title lapses but the supplier will become a co-owner, with the buyer, of the newly formed goods;

(vi) by *confusio* if the goods are blended or intermingled with other goods so that the independent goods can no longer be identified, and such other goods are to be regarded as the principal goods.[15] If the goods are combined with other goods and neither may be regarded as the principal goods, the retention of title lapses but the supplier will become a co-owner, with the buyer, of the newly formed goods;

(vii) by *specificatio* if the goods lose their independent identity because they are used to form new goods with an entirely new identity.[16] It is not possible to agree that a retained title to raw materials will remain vested in the finished product. If the buyer is acting on his own behalf in forming the new goods, the buyer will, generally speaking, become the absolute owner of the newly formed goods.

Recourse by the buyer's creditors

In principle, the buyer's interest in goods to which the supplier has retained title is not subject to recourse by the buyer's creditors. If these creditors attach or levy execution against such goods, the supplier may challenge the attachment or execution pursuant to Article 456 of the Code of Civil Procedure. Creditors of the buyer who have a right of retention in respect of goods to which title has been retained by the supplier represent an exception to the rule that such goods are not subject to recourse by the buyer's creditors. A right of retention is a right to retain the goods until certain claims in respect thereof are satisfied. An example of a creditor with such a right is a mechanic who has repaired the goods and has not yet been paid. Such a creditor may refuse to deliver the goods, even to the supplier with a retained title, until his claim is satisfied, provided that the buyer had the power to enter into the agreement with the creditor, or the creditor had no reason to doubt the buyer's authority to do so. If the buyer goes bankrupt, the right of retention remains valid[17] and the creditor has

---

[15] Article 5:15.

[16] Article 5:16.

[17] Article 60 (1) Bankruptcy Act.

priority over the supplier with a retained title, insofar as necessary to obtain satisfaction of his claim.

Retention of title and bankruptcy. The buyer's bankruptcy does not, in principle, affect the supplier's right to demand the return of goods to which he has retained title, since these goods do not fall within the buyer's bankruptcy estate. However, pursuant to Article 63a of the bankruptcy Act, the bankruptcy judge may impose a "cooling off period" on all third parties or on certain specific third parties, which means that such third parties may not exercise their rights against the goods without the authorisation of the bankruptcy judge for a period not exceeding one month. The cooling off period affords the trustee time to assess the status of the estate, and may be extended by one month. If a supplier with retained title is affected by a cooling off period, the goods may only be returned to him after the period has lapsed.

After the cooling off period, or earlier if no cooling off period has been ordered, the supplier may request that the trustee declare whether he wishes to honour the agreement and, by paying the sum due, make the goods part of the bankruptcy estate. The trustee may decide to do so if this would be advantageous to the estate, for instance because part of the purchase price has already been paid or because he needs the goods to continue production and wishes to do so. If the trustee decides to honour the agreement, the supplier will enjoy a privileged position in comparison to the other creditors since he will receive either full payment or, at the very least, security for his claim. If the trustee does not make the requested declaration, or does not do so in a timely fashion, the trustee loses the right to himself demand performance of the agreement.[18] If the trustee decides not to honour the agreement, the supplier may, by invoking the retention of clause, effectuate the agreement's rescission. If the goods are still present and identified, the supplier may demand their return. If not, the supplier will have a mere unsecured claim for damages in lieu thereof, based on Article 37a of the Bankruptcy Act.

If the supplier is declared bankrupt before the buyer has performed his obligations, it could perhaps be argued based on Article 35 (1) of the Bankruptcy Act that title cannot thereafter pass to the buyer.[19] In that

---

18 Article 37 Bankruptcy Act.

19 Section 35 (1) provides, in rough translation: "If, on the date of bankruptcy, not all of the acts necessary to effectuate a transfer by the bankrupt have occurred, a valid transfer is no longer possible."

event, the buyer would be unable to obtain title to the goods despite having fulfilled his contractual obligations. Generally speaking, that argument has been rejected on the grounds that since all acts necessary to effectuate a transfer by the supplier have already occurred, Article 35 (1) of the Bankruptcy Act does not apply.

Special position of tax authorities. If the tax authorities have a claim against the buyer, their position is different from that of other creditors in that they enjoy special attachment powers with respect to certain types of property. Pursuant to these powers, the tax authorities are entitled to seize all goods located at the tax debtor's premises which function as furnishings or equipment, that is, not stock in trade, even if such goods are owned by third parties. The only way in which the supplier with a retained title can protect himself against such an attachment by the tax authorities is to remove the goods from the buyer's premises in time. The fact that the buyer is declared bankrupt after the tax authorities levy their attachment does not affect the tax authorities' right to seize goods to which the supplier has retained title, since such goods do not fall within the buyer's bankruptcy estate.

If the supplier demands the return of the goods, the buyer has a claim for restitution of payments he has already made. It is generally accepted that he has a right of retention as security for this claim.[20] The buyer does not lose this retention right as a result of the supplier's bankruptcy.[21] The buyer will often be expressly authorised to sell the goods to which the supplier has retained title, provided that they are intended for resale to third parties in the ordinary course of business. However, this authority terminates in the event the buyer is declared bankrupt or is granted a moratorium, since bankruptcy puts an end to the buyer's ordinary course of business. The trustee may only dispose of the goods if it can reasonably be expected that their purchase price can be paid to the supplier.

Retention of title clauses and contract structure

Retention of title clauses are almost always included in general sales conditions, which may be drawn up by an individual supplier or by a body representing an entire industry or line of business for all companies within that sector. Since parties often refer to their own general conditions in

---

20 Article 6:52 and 57.

21 Article 60 Bankruptcy Act.

making or accepting an offer, situations may arise in which the offer and the acceptance refer to separate general conditions which differ to such an extent that a conflict arises as to which conditions apply to the transaction. Pursuant to case law, a party accepting an offer who wishes to avoid being bound by general conditions referred to in the offer must explicitly reject the application of the general conditions. With respect to divergent sales and purchase conditions, Article 6:225(3) provides: if the offer and acceptance refer to different general conditions, the second reference shall have no effect if it does not expressly reject the applicability of the general conditions indicated in the first reference.

Private international law aspects

Dutch courts make a distinction between the law applicable to the contractual aspects of a retention of title clause (for example, its formation, validity, and interpretation) and that applicable to the consequences of a retention of title clause for the parties' ownership rights in the goods sold, that is, the property law aspects of title retention. The conflict of law rules applicable to the contractual aspects of a retention of title clause are those set forth in the Convention on the Law Application to Contractual Obligations. In the case of an international sale to which the Vienna Sales Convention is applicable,[22] the rules set forth in that Convention govern the contractual aspects of the retention of title clause, except for its validity. The contractual law aspects of a retention of title clause include the issue of whether, in the event of a battle of forms, a retention of title was in fact agreed upon by the parties. The general conflict of law rule applicable to the property law aspects of retention of title is *lex rei sitae*. Under this rule, the law governing a property right in goods is that of the place where the goods are situated at the time the property right comes into existence.

A retention of title clause, despite its limitations, is a useful security device for suppliers of goods seeking to protect their claim for payment. Provided that the buyer still has the goods, and that they can be identified, it should allow the supplier to repossess them, even in the event of the buyer's insolvency, if the buyer fails to fulfil his obligations. With respect to goods such as raw materials or component parts, a retention of title

---

22 The Convention applies to contracts for the sale of goods between parties whose places of business are in different States: (a) when the States are Contracting States; or (b) when the rules of private international law lead to the application of the law of a Contracting State. The Netherlands is a Contracting State.

clause will be extinguished when new goods are formed, although under certain circumstances the supplier will become a co-owner of the newly formed goods.

The author wishes to express his thanks to Els Steenis and Sandra Dixon for their assistance in preparing this chapter.

10 Norway

KNUT BACHKE

Introduction

Under Norwegian law the right of retention of possession is normally a legal right arising out of statute or custom. The right of retention may also be established by contract between the owner and creditor although such agreements are rare as they are not practical under Norwegian law. In respect of the retention of title clause the following arguments are often proffered in support of such a right under Norwegian law: first, this imposes on both parties a pressure to perform the contract since the debtor does not receive the counter-performance without completing his own performance; second, retention of title provides the parties with security in their own performance because the goods need not be delivered until the counter-performance (payment of the price) is simultaneously fulfilled. It is therefore in the case of delay in payment that retention of title applies in Norwegian law and an analogy is drawn with the possessory lien. Thus a right of retention must be limited in terms of its scope and the Norwegian Sale of Goods Act[1] provides that the retention can "secure" satisfaction of the claim. Where there has been delivery the right of detention is lost. In order for the seller in such a situation to be able recover the goods, he must have made a reservation to that effect, but in such a case he is not exercising his right of retention but rather recovery of the object is made pursuant to other rules, notably, distraint or sales lien.

The Basis and Scope of Retention of Title

In principle, all movables whether they have any financial value or not may be subject to retention of title under Norwegian law. However, in respect of movables that can be recorded in Norwegian real property registers the retention of title is protected through registration. In contrast, in respect of some assets, notably ships, a legal right of retention arising out of statute has been accepted in order to provide full security for shipyards in carrying out their work of repairing ships. This can be justified on the basis that the

[1] S.42, Sale of Goods Act, 13 May 1988, No.27.

repairs have often increased the value of the ship to the same extent as the amounts secured by the retention of title clause. Nevertheless, there are important limitations in terms of the types of movables that cannot be retained, for example, Norwegian rules of public law required the debtor to retain certain objects such as passports or a driver's licence.[2]

The principal requirement for the exercise of a retention right under Norwegian law is that of possession. The requirement of possession is, however, not usually formulated so strictly that the creditor must have the object under his physical control. What is essential is that the owner, that is, the debtor has been deprived of control. The traditional formulation of this requirement is that the object in question must physically have been removed from the owner's sphere of control. It is possible under Norwegian law to exchange the object secured if the object originally detained is needed by the debtor. If the party retaining the object accepts the new object as security then few problems arise. Provided the new security is equivalent to the original and the legal protection of the new right is established before the retained object is released then the transaction cannot be avoided under s.5-7 of the Creditors Recovery Act. It should be noted that there are provisions, for example, under the Sale of Goods Act[3] which give the owner a right to enforce exchange of security where the value of the object is disproportionately great in terms of the sums secured.

An important requirement for a valid retention of title provision under Norwegian law is that there must be a "natural" connection between the claim and what is being detained. One cannot in principle retain more than what is necessary to secure the claim, and this claim must have arisen as a consequence of, for example, a failure to pay for the detained object. Where the creditor wishes to extend legal title retention to cover other sums then this is dealt with in terms of possessory lien under Norwegian law.

If and so long as the necessary possession exists, the right of retention is fully protected against the owner's creditors and later contract acquirers of the retained object. Acquisition in good faith cannot occur without the acquirer having had the object delivered and consequently the right of retention is safe so long as the object is in the possession of the person exercising it. In bankruptcy so long as the retained object in itself covers

---

2 S. 24 (1), Road Traffic Act, 18 June 1965, No.4.

3 S.64 (2), Sale of Goods Act, 13 May 1988, No.27.

the claim, the right of retention provides full satisfaction of both principal and interest due.[4] Satisfaction of any balance due must be sought in the debtor's estate and will then give rise to a dividend.[5]

Title retention does not convey any general sales right as does normally a mortgage. Still, the creditor may in some cases be granted a right of sale. This may be in the form of an emergency sale, where the owner cannot pay and the creditor risks being left with the object for an unfavourably long time. This is especially so in cases where the object is perishable such as fresh food. In some situations the creditor may be authorised by statute to sell goods and in this respect the Sales Rights Act 1953 provides for such a right if a tradesman is left with objects that have been ordered but not collected within a certain period.

---

4 S.1-5b Liens Act, 8 February 1980, No.2.

5 S.8-17, Creditors Recovery Act, 8 June 1984, No.59.

11 Portugal

RUI PEIXOTO DUARTE

Introduction

Under Portuguese law the transmission of property operates as an effect of the contract of sale of goods whereby the seller becomes obligated to deliver the goods and the buyer is obligated to pay the agreed price. Retention of title clauses provide an exception to the normal rule that property passes on delivery notwithstanding that risk will have passed at that time. Article 409 of the Portuguese Civil Code facilitates the creation of retention of title clauses in sale contracts in that a seller may as a matter of law reserve the title in goods until the buyer has fully or partially executed his contractual obligations or until another specified event has occurred. In the case of real property or a registrable chattel, Article 409 provides that the retention of title clause must be included in the deed of registration if it is to bind third parties.

The general effect of a sale subject to a reservation of title clause under Portuguese law is that the buyer accepts all the risks that are normally those of the owner of the goods whilst the seller enjoys a quasi security interest in the goods. Should the buyer fail to make his payments, the seller may stipulate a reasonable period of time by which all moneys owed by the buyer have to be paid and that a failure in this respect will constitute a breach of contract. In this circumstance the seller may choose one of two means to protect his position, either the enforced execution of the contract or its rescission. In the first case the seller will seek a court order demanding payment whereas in the case of rescission the seller will notify the buyer of his decision to rescind the contract whereby the buyer is compelled to return the goods to the seller and the seller is required to return any payments the buyer may have made. The seller who opts for rescission is entitled to be compensated for any loss or damages he may have further suffered arising out of the decreased value of the sale, for example, the cost of carriage and packaging. Further in the case of rescission the seller may stipulate a liquidated damages clause although in the case of instalment sale agreements Portuguese legislation sets a ceiling as to the amount that the seller may claim.

Scope of Retention of Title Clauses

In the absence of a specific provision for retention of title in the sales contract ownership of the goods is transferred to the buyer on delivery. The clause stipulating the retention of title must be expressly incorporated in the contract of sale. The form of the clause is subject to legal formalities, for example, in the case of a contract for the purchase and sale of a building this must be enacted as a Deed before a Notary Public and then registered. In the case of registrable chattels the effect of non-registration is that the retention of title clauses will not apply against third parties. Lack of registration, however, may not be relied upon in terms of contractual validity *inter partes* nor can it deprive the seller of his right to rescission. Even where Portuguese law does not require the contract to be in writing it is preferable for reasons of legal certainty to incorporate the retention of title clause in this way. The Supreme Court of Justice in its judgment of 1 March 1979 ruled that retention of title could not be inferred from a clause that stated that the risks of usage of a good would be insured, by means of an insurance policy, in favour of the seller until the full price of the goods had been paid, nor from another clause according to which the transfer of ownership in an aeroplane would only be registered after payment in full.

In spite of the well-established principle of contractual freedom within the limits of the Law, extended retention of title clauses as seen in other countries have not appeared before the Portuguese Courts. Certain academic writers consider that clauses which vertically extend the concept of retention of title to proceeds or to new goods are valid so long as they can be identified. Other academic commentators consider that where the object of the retention of title clause is to retain title in a finished product made from goods supplied then such a clause is void. The argument here is based upon the principle of the unity of the object sold and in the distinction between real rights and rights in proceeds.

Retention of title clauses and insolvency

This is regulated by the provisions of the Code of Special Procedures for the Recovery of Companies and for Insolvency of 1993. According to this legislation, a company is considered to be insolvent when it lacks resources of its own and the necessary credit to meet its financial obligations on time. The declaration of insolvency immediately bars the bankrupt individual, or in the case of an insolvent company, the directors of the company from administering and disposing of its present and future assets. These assets come under escrow and are subject to the management and disposal of an administrative receiver appointed by the court and who acts as the bankrupt's representative for all patrimonial purposes relating to insolvency.

The retention of title clause establishes priority over preferential creditors as regards the assets of an insolvent company. The policy justification for this is one of fairness because why should other creditors benefit equally from the value of the goods supplied subject to retention of title which would not otherwise have been supplied to the debtor? Under the 1993 Law, in order for the seller to enjoy priority over all the creditors of the buyer the total value of the goods delivered subject to a retention of title must be stipulated in writing. The effect of bankruptcy or insolvency upon the contract of sale subject to a retention of title clause does not automatically terminate the contract and the receiver has the option of affirming the contract upon payment of the price.

12 Spain

ALFONSO AREITIO

Introduction

The conventional position under Spanish law is that where goods have been the object of a real or symbolic delivery property will pass. Even so, a retention of title clause incorporated into the sales contract can qualify the agreement. Further, by virtue of the *Law 50/1965, Sale of Goods by Instalments* the retention of title clause can be registered at the Special Registry and this was ruled by the *Ministerial Order, 15 May 1982* to be effective against third parties so long as the clause is embodied in a written contract in accordance with Articles 1227 and 1228 of the Civil Code. The nature of a retention of title clause is that the seller maintains the ownership in the goods until full payment of the price and such a clause has been upheld by the Supreme Court in numerous decisions 11th July 1983, 19th May 1989, 23rd April 1990, 23rd October 1991, 10th May 1990, 17th June 1992. In so doing the Supreme Court is reflecting the contractual liberty principle which is reflected in Article 1255 of the Civil Code.

The Basis and Scope of Retention of Title

This is difficult to state. The retention of title clause is sometimes categorised as a purchase agreement with a deferred execution of the obligations but this is hard to sustain since it appears to break the link between the creation and execution of the agreement. At other times, the retention of title clause has been categorised as a suspensive condition whereby title will only pass when the condition (full payment) is fulfilled. This has been criticised on the basis that it does not cohere with the intention of the seller and, furthermore, it does not explain the legal position of the buyer. Another approach is to draw an analogy between retention of title and the *Ley de Hipoteca Mobiliaria y Prenda sin Desplazamiento* (the law of Chattel Mortgage and Pledge without Transmission of the Possession) of 16th December 1954. This opinion is based on the similar treatment (in terms of legal consequences) which apply to both, namely, risk is deemed to have passed,[1] there are similar obligations in respect of custody and also compensation where goods have been lost or destroyed. This analogy whilst superficially attractive has been criticised on the basis that this does not represent the intention of the seller.

The capacity in which the buyer holds the goods during the intermediate time between delivery and full payment is problematical under Spanish law. Sometimes the buyer in the contract will be described as a simple commodatory but this is not appropriate because the *commodatum* is in essence a gratuitous contract and, as such, does not imply the purpose of transfer of property. At other occasions the buyer has been categorised as a precarist or simple tenant but the difficulty here is that by the very nature of the contract it is the buyer who decides the fulfilment of the obligations and, thereby, whether property passes under the contract. All of these positions are reflected in the Supreme Court decisions of 10th June 1958 and 11th July 1983. In some cases the buyer has been categorised as a depository as seen in the Supreme Court decisions of 26th January 1976 or 19th October 1982 but this approach can be criticised on the basis that it is inconsistent with the purpose of the contract which is that of a sale of goods. The buyer has also been identified with a lease tenant but the problem here is that the essence of a sale contract subject to a retention of title clause is that it is not merely the transmission of the use and enjoyment of a thing for a certain period. It is for this reason that some authors have categorised the position of the buyer as having an expectancy of property and that during the intermediate period he has a "*sui generis* possession", in other words, a "special" possession as a future owner.

Third party purchasers

It is sometimes contended that if the retention of title clause is registered in the Registry pursuant to Article 23 of *Law 50/1965* then third party acquirers cannot be good faith purchasers by virtue of the fact of registration. It is for this reason that some Spanish commentators have maintained that registration is necessary in order for any retention of title clause to be valid. During the period between delivery and fulfilment of

---

1 Article 333 of the Commercial Code provides that risk passes on delivery or the moment the goods are made available to the buyer, or at the time of the perfection of the contract.

the condition of purchase the position appears to be that neither the original seller nor the purchaser has the faculty of disposition.[2] Further, by virtue of Articles 12 and 13 of the *Law 50/1965* a buyer cannot dispose of the goods until full payment without the written consent of the seller or financier. In this circumstance if the buyer sells the goods then he may have committed an offence of illegal appropriation (*apropiacion indebida*) but in order to establish this the Supreme Court decision of 28th October 1988 requires the existence of criminality and measurable damages.

It should be noted that where a third party wrongfully interferes with the possession of the buyer, the buyer will only be able to claim against the third party with the assistance of the seller. Articles 1124, 1478 and 1484 of the Civil Code place obligations upon the seller in respect of warranty of title, right of possession and freedom from hidden defects. If the seller in this circumstance refuses to assist the buyer then this will amount to a breach of contract entitling the buyer to terminate it.

The scope of retention of title clauses

The simple retention of title clause provides that the seller will retain ownership until the buyer has completely paid the stipulated price as well as interest for the delayed payment. A liquidated damages clause will be upheld so long as it is not penal, that is one which provides for compensation for use and damages. Spanish authors divide retention of title clauses into two main categories: first, horizontally extended clauses; second, vertically extended clauses. These will now be discussed in turn.

Cláusulas de extensión horizontal. A typical example of this is the all moneys clause. This is where goods delivered by the seller remain his property until all debts owed to him are paid. Such a clause is considered void by virtue of Article 1116 of the Civil Code and it is also considered to offend against the principle of good faith in commercial transactions.

Cláusulas de extensión vertical. The main type of clauses in this category are as follows:

(i) A continuing clause where title is retained on sub-sale. This clause will be valid and enforceable unless the goods are initially destined for sub-sale as this is outlawed under the *Law 50/1965.*

---

[2] The Supreme Court decision of 12th March 1993 held that during the period the buyer is paying the instalments the seller will not have the faculty of disposition.

(ii) A prolonged clause and a proceeds of sale clause which extend the retention of title to the proceeds of sub sale or the right to sue the sub buyer for them as well as the goods themselves. In these situations it is obviously prudent to provide that the goods and the proceeds of sale should be kept in a separate account or be in some way identifiable. A proceeds of sale clause is upheld on the basis that it arises out of the registration requirement of retention of title clauses in the Special Registry created under the *Law 50/1965 of Sale of Goods by Instalments* which will bind third parties. In order to achieve such registration it is necessary for the goods to be specifically identifiable and this is a requirement of Article 2 (a) of the Ministerial Order of 15th November 1982.

(iii) Aggregation clauses. In the absence of a contrary intention the Civil Code provides as follows:

(a) *Accessio* is governed by Articles 375 to 380 of the Civil Code. The rule is that in the case of incorporation with other goods, the owner of the main element becomes the owner of the object and all of the acccessories.

(b) *Confusio* and *commixtio* are governed by Articles 381 and 382 of the Civil Code and establish that if the goods of different owners are mixed without the physical characteristics of the goods being affected, the owners of the original goods will become co owners and tenants in common of the admixture. But if one of the owners acts in bad faith he will lose his goods and will be bound to indemnify the owner(s) for any damage caused.

(c) *Specificatio* in respect of which Article 383 of the Civil Code provides that where a new product is created and the supplier's goods lose their identity, title in the (new) goods will pass to the manufacturer.

Whilst the parties can vary the application of the above rules *inter se* such agreements do not bind third parties because *Law 50/1965* only recognises retention of title in respect of goods which can be specifically identified. It follows that such clauses are, in practice, not valid under Spanish law and this analysis is confirmed in the Supreme Court decision of October 27, 1992.

The impact of the insolvency regime

The seller with the benefit of a retention of title clause falls within the category of creditors *ex iure domino*. When the buyer has greater assets than liabilities but cannot face his current obligations the retention of title protects the seller from having to prove in competition with other creditors by virtue of Article 908 of the Commercial Code.[3] In other cases of bankruptcy the seller can resort to the procedure *separatio ex iure domino* whereby the assets are not counted as part of the debtor's assets when they are subject to a retention of title clause although this is subject to the agreement of the Creditors Meeting by virtue of Articles 908 and 909 of the Commercial Code. In the case of sales regulated by the *Law 50/1965* the retention of title must be registered if it is to bind third parties and gain priority by virtue of Articles 1922.2 and 1926.1 of the Civil Code and Article 918 of the Commercial Code if the defaulting party is a merchant. If the retention of title clause is registered the receiver can only acquire the goods by paying the instalments as they become due.

In the case of the seller's insolvency the sales contract will remain effective so long as the buyer makes full payment of the agreed instalments. The vendor's creditors are subrogated to the seller's position in respect of the contract.[4]

International private law considerations

Article 10.5 of the Civil Code recognises the autonomy of will principle and establishes that the contractual obligations will be determined by the parties' express choice of law so long as it is related to the contract. In other cases the applicable law will be the place where the contract has been entered into. Articles 10.1 and 2 of the Civil Code provide that possession, property, publicity and other property rights of real estate property and movable assets will be ruled by the law of the place where the assets are located. This is significant in respect of retention of title of international goods if compliance is to be made with the registration provisions of the *Law 50/1965* and this is confirmed by the decision of the Supreme Court on June 22, 1992.

---

[3] Articles 15 and 22 Supervision of Payments Law.

[4] See also Articles 1124, 1502-1505 Civil Code; Article 11 *Law 50/1965*.

13 Sweden

MATS KOFFNER

Introduction

The concept of title includes a number of different rights for the person who can show that he has title to the asset at issue. As such, title protects the person from a claim by another person in respect of that asset. The dilemma under Swedish law is how can one define title? Probably, this question can only be answered negatively, that is, the owner can only be prevented from exercising his right to utilise the property if he himself has placed limits on the title or that the limitation is a direct result of legislation. Generally speaking, the concept of title is a relative concept which has been formed in accordance with the laws and regulations applying when title is claimed.

The starting point for title is that it is exercised in relation to a specific object. This object is then considered to be the subject of the exercise of title. The division of such an object into smaller units, differentiated title, is rare and it is more common for several persons to exercise joint title to the object. In cases where it appears to be reasonable to detach an identified accession this is a special instance where title is divided. Further, the title to a certain value or quantity of a certain larger amount of goods, for example, a certain number of litres of petrol in a container, devolves upon the buyer when the petrol purchased has been separated from the container. It could be said that prior to this separation, the purchaser of a certain amount of petrol only has a claim to the amount of the petrol.

Under Swedish law, title is regarded as one of the most powerful rights *in rem.* Title includes the right to control and dispose of the property subject only to the restrictions the owner has voluntarily accepted or which have been imposed by legislation. Security rights are usually divided under Swedish law into lien, right of retention, right of retaining lien, right of detention and floating charges. A lien gives the holder of the lien the possibility of utilising the property in possession as a security to ensure that the debt is paid on time. If payment is not made, the asset may be sold to settle the debt. The right of retention refers to the debt. The right of retaining lien refers to the right to withhold property belonging to another person as security for a claim against that person. The right of detention is a right to withhold one's own property pending performance of the obligations of the other contracting party, notably, payment of the price. Floating charges under Swedish law may be granted by natural or legal persons in respect of business assets and this mechanism gives the chargee the right to payment from certain assets held by the chargor, for example, fittings and fixtures, stock and receivables.

The Scope of Retention of Title

The transfer of title is a matter of contractual intention under Swedish law. By virtue of s.54 of the Sale of Goods Act and s.40 of the Consumer Purchases Act, a vendor may cancel the sale if the purchaser delays making payment and the delay constitutes a significant breach. If the buyer has already taken factual possession of the goods, the vendor may cancel the sale only if he has reserved the right to do so or the purchaser rejects the goods. An agreement incorporating the right for the vendor to reclaim the goods does not require any special form but, in practice, it will normally be in writing which is important from an evidential perspective. In any event, an agreement in respect of retention of title must be entered into no later than the time when the goods, the subject of the agreement, are handed over to the purchaser. Further it should be noted that not all property can be included within the scope of an effective retention of title agreement, for example, fixtures cannot be reclaimed if they have been permanently installed in the building of land. This also applies in the case of movable property where the former can be treated as an accessory to the latter. Nor can a retention of title clause be applied in the case of goods that have been used in a manufacturing process or have been consumed in such a process where this was anticipated by the vendor in the supply contract.

Under s.61 of the Sale of Goods Act the vendor is given a right of suspension, that is, the vendor is entitled to stop the property, the subject of the sale, from being delivered to the buyer if it can be shown that there is good reason to assume that the purchaser will fail to fulfil a significant part of his obligations. In this circumstance the vendor is under an obligation to inform the purchaser immediately if the right of suspension of performance is invoked. If the vendor fails to give timeous notice, the purchaser is entitled under Swedish law to compensation for damages caused by the late notice.

Formalities and retention of title

There is no mandatory requirement for registration of retention of title clauses under Swedish law in contrast, for example, to other real rights such as floating charges which are registered in court. In Sweden retention of title clauses have become popular precisely because of this reason and it can be argued that the market has been provided with an instrument which stimulates sales. Thus a trustee in bankruptcy of the buyer will take the goods subject to the retention of title clause and the original vendor may reclaim the goods from the bankrupt's estate. However, where the original vendor is still in possession of the object subject to a retention of title clause, in order to protect the purchaser from the vendor's creditor, a written document covering the purchase must be drawn up and a notice about the purchase must be printed in the local newspaper. This notice must include the names of the vendor and the purchaser, information in respect of the property and the purchase amount. There is a set time in respect of which the agreement and the notice must be shown to the enforcement service authority in the county where the property is located: if this is complied with, the purchaser has the right to reclaim the goods should the vendor become insolvent.

Enforcement

Section 25 of the Consumer Credit Act enables the vendor to rely upon a retention of title clause to resume his right to payment so long as the delay in payment is not insignificant and the property does not fall within the non-distrainable category under the Execution Code. Significantly, s.7 of the Credit Sales Between Undertakings Act provides that retention of title clauses may only be utilised if the purchaser's delay in payment is more than 14 days.

It is important that the goods subject to retention of title can be identified. In the case NJA 1976 s.251, a vendor had sold containers to the purchaser subject to several different hire-purchase contracts. Some of the containers were paid for while others were sold subject to hire-purchase contracts containing a retention of title clause. In its decision, the Court noted that the Hire Purchase Act prohibits retention of title clauses intended to secure payment of a purchase sum for property other than the property to be repossessed. In its majority decision, the Court pointed out that it was impossible to establish which containers were paid for and which had been sold on hire-purchase contracts containing a retention of title clause and that as a consequence of this, the vendor was not permitted to repossess any part of the property he had sold. This case illustrates the importance of clearly being able to distinguish and identify property sold subject to a retention of title clause.

In respect of third party conflicts, retention of title clauses have in Swedish case law been declared to be of no legal consequence where a purchaser has been permitted to dispose of the property before payment. It is otherwise if the purchaser has disposed of the goods contrary to the agreement and the sub-purchaser was not in good faith when he purchased the goods. Where the vendor has permitted resale the proceeds of such sale are not available to the original seller in priority to other creditors.

Private international law considerations

At one level an agreement which includes a retention of title clause should be determined according to the proper law of the contract. However, such claims often involve real property considerations so the *lex rei sitae* principle will apply in respect of both fixed and movable property. A pre-requisite of a retention of title clause agreed on abroad between two parties with regard to property located in Sweden is that such a clause should be valid according to Swedish real property law where third party interests are affected. As discussed above, such a clause will not be valid if a purchaser is entitled to consume the property or he has purchased it to resell it.

14 Switzerland

PHILIPP KÄNZIG

Introduction

Under Swiss law the general principles of retention of title are governed by Article 715 *et seq* of the Swiss Civil Code (CC). The effect of a retention of title clause is that the seller can reserve title in the goods until the buyer has fulfilled certain conditions, notably, full payment of the purchase price and the seller can repossess the goods if the agreed conditions are not met by the buyer. By virtue of Article 715, paragraph 1 CC a retention of title clause is only valid if it is registered in a public register kept by the Debt Collection Office at the domicile of the buyer. Whilst under Swiss law a retention of title clause can be seen in the context of a gift subject to conditions, construction contracts and certain partnership agreements nevertheless, the main area of application is, predominantly, the sale of goods.

In the case of a sale of goods the seller is required to offer the contractually agreed upon goods to the buyer and the buyer is required to accept and pay for the goods as provided for in the contract. In the absence of specific contractual clauses to the contrary the purchase price becomes due and payable at the moment the buyer receives physical possession of the goods.[1] In such cases, a retention of title clause would serve no purpose. If, however, the seller gives the buyer credit for the purchase price by allowing the buyer to pay a part or all of the purchase price at a later date, the situation is different and the purpose of a retention of title clause as a means to secure a credit given to the buyer becomes apparent. If the seller gives possession of the goods to the buyer without a retention of title clause, he relies solely on the creditworthiness of the buyer and his claim for payment gives him only a money cause of action against the buyer. The seller must therefore enforce his claim without any right of preference to the goods he delivered to the buyer. The object of the retention of title clause is to give the seller a preference right in the sold goods to secure the credit he has extended to the buyer until the entire purchase price has been paid or until certain other conditions have been fulfilled.

1 Article 213 of the Swiss Code of Obligations (CO).

The retention of title clause does not give the seller absolute protection. The reason for this is that the retention of title is not implied by law and it must be expressly provided for in the contract between the seller and the buyer and properly registered with the Debt Collection Office at the domicile of the buyer. In the absence of a properly registered agreement between buyer and seller, Article 714 CC provides that ownership of movable goods passes to the buyer with possession of these goods as provided for in Articles 922-925 CC. These provide, as a general rule, that possession is transferred by the previous owner willingly giving the acquirer the means to freely dispose of the acquired goods.[2] Possession can also be transferred by proxy[3] and by way of transfer of documents giving evidence of possession and ownership of goods such as bills of lading.[4] In such cases the transfer of possession of documents of title to the buyer substitutes the transfer of possession of the goods themselves. However, Article 925, paragraph 2 CC provides that if there is a conflict between the recipient of such documents and the recipient of the goods themselves the right of the recipient of the goods will prevail if both recipients were acting in good faith. Further Article 924 CC provides that the acquirer of goods can obtain possession even if the goods themselves remain with the seller or are shipped to a third party by way of an express agreement (*constitutum possessorium*) providing that the seller (or the third party) exercises possession on behalf of the buyer.[5]

The consequence of the rules of possession and ownership outlined above is that the protection offered to the seller by a retention of title clause is not absolute. If, for instance, the buyer breaches his contract with the seller and resells the purchased merchandise to a third party, he will acquire good title in the merchandise so long as he is acting in good faith.[6] The law therefore gives priority to the protection of a party acquiring goods based on the presumption that a person who has possession of movable goods also has title to these goods over and above any protection given to the seller by way of a retention of title clause. Not only is the acquirer of goods protected if he is in good faith, the same also applies to a third party who is a creditor of the buyer and who obtains possession of the acquired goods with the consent of the buyer. For example, if the buyer

---

2 Article 922 CC.

3 Article 923 CC.

4 Article 925 CC.

5 Article 924 CC.

6 Article 714, para.2 in connection with Article 933 CC.

stores his goods in a warehouse belonging to a third party and fails to pay his storage fees, Article 895 CC gives this third party a retention right (a legal lien) which has priority over the retention of title clause between seller and buyer. Furthermore Swiss law expressly provides for such a retention right of the landlord with regard to all movable goods kept in the leased premises by the tenant,[7] it is advisable to inform the landlord of the buyer of the retention of title clause (thereby destroying the landlord's good faith in the legal ownership of the tenant) before the goods are transferred to the premises leased by the buyer. Since Article 3 CC provides that it shall legally be presumed - until proof is brought to the contrary - that a person is acting in good faith, it is advisable to give such a notice in writing.

The risk and benefit in goods sold will in the absence of a different contractual arrangement pass from the seller to the buyer upon conclusion of the contract and not upon the transfer of possession or ownership.[8] Therefore, a retention of title clause in no way prevents the passing of risk and benefit to the buyer. As a consequence, the seller remains entitled to payment notwithstanding the retention of title clause even if the goods perish after the conclusion of the purchase agreement or, in the case of generic goods, after the time the goods are separated from other goods of their kind for the purpose of the consummation of the transaction.[9] In this context it should also be noted that the retention of title clause applies only to the sold goods themselves and not to any replacement of these goods where they have perished entirely or in part.[10]

Retention of Title Clauses: The Legal Background

Article 715, paragraph 1 CC provides, in general, that the parties may agree that ownership shall pass from the seller to the buyer upon complete payment of the purchase price without observing any requirements as to form. However, certain consumer protection laws derogate from this general rule and expressly require an agreement in writing in the case of the sale of goods to private individuals. Since commercial parties will hardly rely on oral undertakings, a written retention of title clause will be

---

[7] Article 268 CO.

[8] Article 185 CO.

[9] Article 185, para.2 CO.

[10] *BGE* (Decision of the Swiss Federal Supreme Court) *88 II 86.*

the rule rather than the exception. In order to avoid the misuse of retention of title clauses to the detriment of other creditors, the Swiss Federal Supreme Court has ruled[11] that the agreement incorporating a retention of title by the seller must be concluded no later than the transfer of possession in the goods.

Registration

A retention of title clause creates an element of risk for third parties who conclude transactions with the buyer in reliance on the buyer's legal title to the goods in his possession. Without registration such third parties have no possibility to verify the title of their contractual partners in the goods they purport to own. This is especially the case in the event of commercial loans which are often extended in reliance upon the assets in the possession of the debtor. Therefore, Article 715, paragraph 1 CC provides that a retention of title clause becomes valid only upon registration in a public register, the Retention of Title Clause Register (RTCR) which is maintained by the Debt Collection Offices in each community. Third parties can consult this register before extending credit or entering into other business relationships and therefore protect their interests.

The retention of title clause must be registered at the domicile of the buyer which in the case of a corporation means its main statutory domicile. In the event of a change of domicile, re-registration at the new domicile is necessary. The registration at the previous domicile expires after three months irrespective of the knowledge of the seller of the change of domicile. The seller must therefore carefully monitor the domicile of any parties who have possession of his goods under a retention of title clause and all buyers should as a matter of contract be obliged to report any change of domicile to the seller during the entire duration of the retention of title agreement. If the seller misses the deadline of three months, full title passes to the buyer; the seller may, however, regain title with effect as of the date of re-registration at the new domicile.[12]

Neither the Civil Code nor the Ordinance of the Federal Supreme Court contain provisions with regard to the time of registration. It has been consistently held by the Swiss Federal Supreme Court that the retention of title clause can be registered at any time before or after the transfer of

---

11 *BGE 93 III 104.*

12 Article 3, paras.1 and 3 of the ordinance of the Swiss Federal Supreme Court regarding the Registration of Retention of Title Clauses (FO).

possession of the goods. However, if possession is transferred before registration, full title passes to the buyer upon the buyer obtaining possession and the seller only has the right to re-obtain title in the goods with effect as of the later date of registration.[13]

Legal effects of Registration. This has only the effect of "negative publicity", that is to say any third party may rely in full on the non-registration of a retention of title agreement. Registration does not have the effect of "positive publicity"; that is, registration does not prove the existence and validity of a retention of title clause. Therefore, a third party purchasing registered goods from the seller will not be protected by a presumption of good faith due to the registration of the seller. As previously indicated, registration of a retention of title clause does not exclude the good faith purchase of the goods from the buyer by a third party. There is no legal presumption that third parties must know the contents of the RTCR. Even so there are limits to the protection afforded to good faith purchasers. The Federal Supreme Court has, in the past, repeatedly applied Article 3, paragraph 2 CC, whereby a person who did not exercise the due diligence which could be expected from him under the circumstances cannot call upon the presumption of good faith in accordance with Article 3, paragraph 1 CC. In BGE 113 II 400 the Federal Supreme Court was called upon to decide, in connection with the sale of used cars, if a professional dealer in used cars is required, in accordance with Article 3, paragraph 2 CC, to consult the RTCR before a purchase. Although the Federal Supreme Court held that in general no such duty exists, the court was of the opinion that in areas with a high risk of fraudulent transactions, such as the used car business, due diligence requires that a dealer consult the RTCR.

Where a retention of title clause has been validly made and registered, the sale of goods by the buyer will constitute an embezzlement in accordance with Article 138 of the Swiss Federal Penal Code. This will be a small consolation to the seller since a retention of title clause does not prevent third parties from obtaining title to the goods so long as they are in good faith.

---

[13] *BGE 93 III 104.*

The scope of retention of title

There is a controversy in Swiss legal literature with regard to the legal definition of a retention of title agreement. Most authors are of the opinion that in the case of a retention of title agreement, title in the goods passes to the buyer with a suspensive condition. Therefore, full title passes to the buyer only upon full payment of the purchase price. However, other authors have argued that a retention of title clause constitutes a resolutive condition whereby title passes to the buyer immediately but under the condition that he pays the full purchase price and with the effect that the seller re-obtains full title if the buyer does not fulfil this obligation. For most questions in connection with retention of title clauses this issue is purely academic. The only real significance of this question is, if, and under which conditions, the seller or the buyer can create a lien in goods which have been sold subject to a retention of title clause. Following the prevailing doctrine of a suspensive condition, the seller remains entitled to create a lien with regard to goods he has sold under a retention of title clause. However, in doing so, he will, in most cases, violate his agreement with the buyer, thus giving the buyer a claim for damages and a legal lien in the goods as security for this claim. Therefore the creation of a lien by the seller will, in practice, be effective only if the buyer has agreed to the creation of the lien or if the buyer does not comply with the terms and conditions of the purchase agreement, thereby allowing the seller to exercise his right to repossess the goods.

Subject matter. According to Article 715 CC all movable goods with the exception of cattle and ships can be the subject matter of a retention of title clause. With regard to perishable goods such clauses are legally possible but title will only remain with the seller with respect to the goods which have not yet been used or which have not yet perished. Article 715, paragraph 3 provides that cattle cannot be sold under a retention of title arrangement. Horses, cows, mules, donkeys, sheep, goats and pigs may, however, be sold subject to a lien of the seller in accordance with Article 885 CC. Such a lien - which is not permitted by law with regard to other movable goods - protects the interest of the seller far better than a retention of title clause with all of its uncertainties. A retention of title clause is also excluded with regard to ships which are registered in a Cantonal or Federal ship's register. In these cases, the possibility of a lien also exists.

Expiry of the retention of title clause. This occurs following its deletion from the RTCR. According to Article 12, paragraph 1 CO the deletion of a retention of title clause can be requested orally or in writing by the seller. The deletion can also be requested by the buyer with the consent of the seller or in conjunction with a valid and binding judgment replacing the seller's consent. The retention of title clause also expires, without its deletion from the register, under the following circumstances: first, complete payment of the purchase price or fulfilment of all conditions connected with the retention of title clause by the buyer; second, the change of domicile of the buyer if the retention of title clause is not registered at the new domicile of the buyer within 3 months; third, the *bona fide* purchase of the goods by a third party; fourth, if the goods become part of other goods; fifth, with regard to goods which have been used up or which have perished. In the event that movable goods subject to a retention of title clause become part of other goods, for example, by accession, the retention of title clause loses its effect.[14]

Effects of retention of title outside of insolvency procedures

If goods are sold and the seller gives the buyer credit for the purchase price, the consequences of an event of default are governed by the Code of Obligations. According to Article 102, paragraph 1 CO the seller must give the buyer notice of an event of default. This requirement is deemed to be waived if a specific date of performance was expressly agreed upon. Once the buyer is in default, the seller may alternatively continue to demand performance of the contract[15] or rescind the contract and demand compensation for damages suffered through the rescission of the contract.[16] Article 214, paragraph 3 CO provides that if the seller applies the general rule of Articles 107/109 CO to a contract concerning the sale of goods, he may only demand the return of the sold goods if this was expressly agreed upon in the contract. A retention of title clause in the contract, whether the clause is registered or not, is deemed to be such an agreement in accordance with Article 214, paragraph 3 CO.[17] In the event that a valid retention of title clause exists, the seller is not required to give the buyer an opportunity to remedy the default.

---

[14] Article 642 CC, *BGE 76 II 28.*

[15] Article 107, para.2 CO.

[16] Article 107, para.2 and Article 109 CO.

[17] *BGE 90 II 292.*

Where goods are sold in connection with an agreement to pay the purchase price in instalments, the principles outlined above generally apply. The following special provision must, however, also be observed. First, in addition to the two possibilities outlined above, the seller may also demand immediate payment of the entire amount still outstanding; second, the seller may only rescind the contract, if the buyer is in default with at least two instalments in the aggregate amount of at least 10 per cent of the purchase price or with one instalment in the amount of at least 25 per cent of the purchase price; third, if the purchase agreement is a consumer contract, the seller is obliged to give the buyer a deadline of at least 14 days to remedy the event of default; fourth, if the seller rescinds the purchase contract and demands the return of the goods from the buyer, he may do so only against repayment to the buyer of those instalments of the purchase price which the buyer has already paid following deduction of an amount which is adequate to account for rent and wear and tear.[18] The buyer has a legal lien in the goods for this claim.[19]

Retention of title clauses in insolvency procedures

We have seen that under Swiss law a retention of title agreement between the buyer and seller will not protect the seller against the fraudulent acts of the buyer, notably, the sale of the goods by the buyer to a third party acting in good faith. Under Swiss law the main purpose and the main effect of a retention of title clause is to protect the seller in case of insolvency of the buyer. The Swiss Federal Statute on Debt Collection and Bankruptcy (DCB) provides for three different insolvency procedures depending on the legal status of the debtor. In the event that the debtor is a private person, claims are enforced by the Debt Collection Office seizing those assets of the debtor which are not necessary to provide the debtor with a minimal standard of living and selling these assets in a forced auction. For the debtor this procedure does not constitute a relief since he continues to remain liable to all his creditors until his debts have been fully settled. Therefore, it is becoming more frequent for private individuals to voluntarily submit to bankruptcy procedures. If the debtor is a corporation, claims are enforced by way of bankruptcy procedures. In such bankruptcy procedures a receiver is appointed (in most cases an officer of the Bankruptcy Office) who proceeds to sell all of the debtor's assets. In the

---

[18] Article 226, para.1 CO, and Article 716 CC.

[19] Article 195 CC.

course of this procedure, the debtor company is liquidated. If a private individual voluntarily submits to bankruptcy procedures all his assets not necessary for a certain minimal standard of living are also sold, the debtor does, however, have the possibility to make a new start and his creditors are severely restricted in the possibility of later collecting anything with regard to old debts which were not settled in the course of the bankruptcy procedure. As a third possibility, Swiss law provides in respect to both companies and to private individuals the possibility of a reorganisation under the Bankruptcy Act. Such a reorganisation does, however, requires the approval of both the court and a majority of creditors.

Retention of title clauses and debt collection procedures. Goods subject to a valid retention of title agreement are brought to a public auction by the Debt Collection Office but they can only be sold in the auction if a price is achieved which fully covers the claim of the seller to the outstanding amount of the purchase price. If this price is not achieved the seller may demand that his title be respected and repossess the goods sold subject to the retention of title clause. In this case the seller must yield to the claim of the buyer exercised through the Debt Collection Office in favour of other creditors for repayment of the portion of the purchase price which has already been paid by the buyer with a deduction being made taking into account wear and tear and loss of profit.

According to Article 96, paragraph 2 DCB the debtor loses all rights to dispose of his assets upon their seizure by the Debt Collection Office. Therefore, the debtor may no longer transfer ownership of or liens in seized assets to third parties. If a retention of title clause is registered after the seizure of the assets concerned (by either the buyer or the seller or both), the rights of creditors to be satisfied out of the results of the forced auction have priority over the rights of the seller under the retention of title clause. Third parties who nevertheless acquire ownership over such seized assets in good faith in accordance with the rules of possession are, again, protected so long as they are in good faith. It therefore remains to be examined if the seller who repossesses seized goods based on a retention of title clause which has not been registered and who is in good faith and without knowledge of the seizure by the Debt Collection Office can be protected. The answer to this question is to be found in the legal nature of the registration of a retention of title clause. Without registration, the retention of title clause does not exist and the seller who repossesses goods therefore acts without a "cause" for repossession. In such a case, the rights of the ordinary creditors of the buyer must also prevail and the seller must return the assets to the Debt Collection Office for forced auction.[20]

Retention of title clauses in bankruptcy procedures. The position is very similar to the situation in Debt Collection Procedures. If a reservation of title clause is registered before the buyer is declared bankrupt, the seller has the right to repossess his assets if the receiver does not agree to fully satisfy the claim of the seller for the remaining portion of the purchase price. Again repossession is, however, only possible if the seller repays the portion of the purchase price already paid by the buyer after deduction of an amount adequate to account for wear and tear and loss of profit. With regard to registration of a retention of title clause after the buyer has been declared bankrupt, the situation is also very similar to the situation in debt collection procedures. According to Article 204, paragraph 1 DCB all acts of the debtor with regard to assets subject to the bankruptcy procedure are invalid in relation to the other creditors. The seller can therefore not gain anything by registering the retention of title clause after the buyer has been declared bankrupt. The only exception to this rule is that a retention of title clause can still be registered with regard to goods which are exempt from bankruptcy procedures because they are necessary for the debtor to maintain his guaranteed minimal standard of living.[21]

Retention of title clauses in the case of reorganisation. Swiss law provides for the three different forms of reorganisation. The most frequent form is reorganisation by liquidation in agreement with the creditors.[22] In this case the situation is similar to formal bankruptcy procedures and the retention of title clause cannot be registered after the court has granted the debtor a stay to file his petition for reorganisation. If the retention of title clause was registered in a timely manner, the seller has the same rights as in bankruptcy procedures. In the other two cases of reorganisation, the debtor is not liquidated and the unsecured creditors accept either a reduction of their claims[23] or a stay in favour of the debtor. In both cases a retention of title clause can still be registered during reorganisation procedures and the seller retains all rights he would otherwise have.

---

20 Decision of the Civil Court of Basel-Stadt published in *Schweizerische Juristen Zeitung 59* (1963) p.113 *et seq.*

21 Article 92 DCB.

22 Article 317 *et seq.* DCB.

23 Article 314 DCB.

Private international law considerations

Article 102, paragraph 2 of the Swiss Federal International Private Law Statute (IPLS) provides for the continuing validity of a retention of title clause created abroad for a period of three months after the goods concerned have been imported into Switzerland. Within this period of three months the seller has the possibility to register a retention of title clause which was validly created in a foreign jurisdiction. If the contract is subject to a foreign law, the only condition for registration is that a retention of title agreement under the foreign law is materially equivalent to a retention of title agreement under Swiss law. Again, if the seller misses the three months deadline, he may still register his retention of title clause at a later date with effect as of this later date. Article 102, paragraph 2 IPLS does not provide for the case that goods sold by a seller domiciled abroad temporarily pass through Swiss territory. In such cases the prevailing opinion in legal literature is that a retention of title clause is valid and binding if it is valid under the laws of either the seller's or the buyer's domicile. Further, the IPLS does not take into account the possibility that goods could be sold under a retention of title clause by a seller domiciled abroad to a buyer domiciled abroad for delivery to Switzerland. Such a retention of title clause could not, according to the law, be registered in Switzerland because the buyer does not have a domicile in Switzerland. In practice the retention of title clause can, in such cases, be registered at the Debt Collection Office of the place in Switzerland where the goods are located. Lastly, Article 103 IPLS provides that a retention of title clause shall, in the case of goods destined for export, be governed by the law of the destination of the goods. Registration with a Swiss Debt Collection Office is therefore not necessary.

Article 102, paragraph 3 IPLS provides that the principle of good faith shall override a (valid) retention of title clause created under a foreign law but not yet registered with the appropriate Swiss Debt Collection Office. Since even registration does not prevent the valid acquisition of title by a third party acting in good faith this provision can only mean that good faith creditors in debt collection or bankruptcy procedures will also be protected. Therefore, until a foreign retention of title clause has been registered in Switzerland its only effect is that it must be observed by third parties who have knowledge thereof and that it remains valid as between the buyer and the seller. It is therefore advisable to immediately register the retention of title clause notwithstanding the three months grace period.

Due to the strict formal requirements and the limited protection offered to the seller, retention of title agreements do not have great potency in Switzerland. In the case of consumer goods, sellers have found that the administrative burden of registering such clauses and of monitoring the domicile of their buyers is such that there is very little benefit in such agreements. Therefore, whilst most contracts of sale of goods on credit contain a retention of title clause, the sellers, in practice, rarely go to the trouble of registering the clause with the Debt Collection Office. In the case of commercial transactions the registration of retention of title clauses is not unusual; however, the seller will rarely solely rely on a retention of title clause and will additionally require security in the form of guarantees and/or liens on other property of the buyer. If a seller, especially a foreign seller, supplies goods on credit to a Swiss buyer in reliance on a retention of title clause he will, in all cases, be well advised to register his right with the appropriate Debt Collection Office before sending the goods to the buyer.

15 United Kingdom

IWAN DAVIES

Introduction

The effect of a retention of title clause is a sale of goods subject to a condition precedent usually connected with the payment of the price. Sections 17 and 19 of the English and Scottish Sale of Goods Act 1979 (as amended) provide that property passes in goods when the parties intend, that is, it is determined by contract rather than conveyance. In the absence of an express intention s.18 rule 1 of the Act states that in the case of "an unconditional contract for the sale of specific goods in a deliverable state, the property in the goods passes to the buyer when the contract is made." It follows from this that (in the absence of a contrary intention) even when a supplier of goods allows the buyer a period of credit, property in the goods will pass to the buyer at the time the contract is made.

Reservation of title clauses are not a new phenomenon in England and Wales. Indeed it was the ingenuity of Victorian Commercial Lawyers which provided for the hire purchase mechanism, that is a bailment of goods with an option to purchase. It was the decision of the Court of Appeal in *Aluminium Industrie Vaassen BV* v *Romalpa Aluminium Ltd* [1] which alerted the English and Scottish commercial world of the benefits which can flow to a supplier who has sold goods subject to a retention of title clause. One legal counsel in that case referred to it as the most important case for 25 years and doubted whether any case this century in the U.K. has had a greater impact on the British commercial world. The facts involved a Dutch plaintiff who had supplied the defendant company quantities of aluminium foil. The terms of supply stated that ownership of the materials transferred to the buyer only once the buyer had met all sums owing to the supplier. The terms further allowed the buyer to use the goods in the production of other products and to sell on those new products on the condition that the defendants would, on request, assign their rights against their sub-purchasers to the plaintiffs. The defendants encountered financial difficulties and had a receiver appointed. The court held that not only were the plaintiffs entitled to a quantity of the foil supplied by them

[1] [1976] 1 WLR 676.

and which was held by the defendants at the date of the receiver's appointment but they were also entitled to certain proceeds of sale which had been received by the defendants by that date from the sub-purchasers of goods containing the foil supplied by the plaintiffs.

Such is the significance of *Aluminium Industrie Vaassen BV* v *Romalpa Aluminium Ltd* that retention of title clauses are often simply referred to as "Romalpa" clauses. The passing (or reservation) of title carries various consequences under the Act, of which two are worthy of note at this point. Firstly, by virtue of s.20, risk in the goods will, in the absence of contrary agreement, pass to the buyer on delivery and as a consequence this will require him to insure the goods. Secondly, under s.49 (1), the seller may maintain an action for the price of the goods once property in the goods has passed to the buyer. It is common practice to provide in a *Romalpa* clause that the seller may sue for the price notwithstanding that title has not transferred to the buyer.

Retention of Title Clauses: The Legal Background

The emphasis on property reservation is that it allows the owner to seize the property should the debtor fail in one of his primary obligations. In a sense virtually all extensions of credit give the creditor a contingent right to take property of the debtor in order to limit the extent of the indebtedness, that is, after a court judgment the creditor can 'execute' or 'levy' on some of the debtor's property in order to satisfy the judgment. While the secured creditor has the right not enjoyed by the unsecured creditor to take property without the post-default consent of the debtor and without going to court, this may not be so valuable outside liquidation and even sometimes at liquidation, because a debtor's active objection will require the secured creditor to go to court as well. Reservation of title clause gives suppliers the opportunity of obtaining priority over secured creditors in the event of the buyer's insolvency. That priority is by way of a retained ownership interest and not merely a security interest in terms of legal categorisation. Nevertheless in terms of economic effect, a retention of title clause operates in the nature of a charge over the goods in favour of the seller. However, whilst its effect is as a security, its form is not that of a charge but merely as a term of the contract of sale under which title is reserved. This distinction between mere reservation of title and the creation of a charge is of relevance to the validity of retention of title clauses. In particular, s.62 (4) of the Sale of Goods Act 1979 specifically provides that the provisions of the Act do not apply to a transaction "in the form of a contract of sale which is intended to operate by way of mortgage, pledge, charge or other security". This provision was originally introduced into the Sale of Goods legislation to deal with a particular problem of Scots law which does not recognise security rights over movable property unless possession of those goods also passes to the security holder. Even so, s.62 (4) applies not only to Scotland but also to England and Wales and its effect is that if a retention of title clause is considered to amount to a charge, instead of a sale, the transaction will be treated as outside the scope of the Sale of Goods Act. The relevance of this is that the creation of most charges granted by companies require registration under the Companies Act 1985 as a pre-requisite of their enforceability. By contrast, pure retention of title clauses are not subject to registration. Great care, therefore, is required in drafting an enforceable retention of title clause.

Registration of company charges

Section 395 of the Companies Act 1985 provides that certain charges created by a company registered in England and Wales will be void against the liquidator, administrator and any creditor of the company unless prescribed particulars of the charge are delivered to the Registrar of Companies for registration within 21 days after the date of creation of the charge. The charges to which this section applies include a charge created or evidenced by an instrument which, if executed by an individual, would require registration as a bill of sale; a charge on book debts of the company; and a floating charge on the company's undertaking or property.[2] Detailed comment on the bills of sale legislation is unnecessary here, but a person granting a charge over goods by way of security or selling goods while remaining in possession may have to register the bill of sale effecting the transaction. The equivalent Scottish provision[3] covers securities over certain kinds of incorporeal movable property, such as book debts, and also floating charges. As in England and Wales any such charge which has not been registered within 21 days of creation will be void against a liquidator, administrators and creditors. In short, therefore, many forms of company charges require registration.

---

2 S.396 (1), Companies Act, 1985.

3 S.410, Companies Act, 1985.

Reservation of title clauses, as such, are not subject to registration under the existing legislation. However, the registration requirements, in fact pose a significant difficulty for the more complicated forms of clause insofar as they are construed to constitute to charges. Where a clause amounts to a charge, failure to register the clause, or the relevant part of it, will result in the charge element of it being invalid. However, to attempt to register a retention of title clause is unlikely to prove straightforward. Technical problems may arise in ascertaining with certainty when such a "charge" arises and the need to register a "charge" for each and every sale is likely to be an administrative nightmare.

A basic distinction is drawn in companies legislation between charges created by a company and charges existing on property which have been acquired by the company in question. Whilst both categories of charges are registrable, there is a significant difference as regards the consequences of non-registration. In the case of a charge which is already subsisting on property that is acquired by the company, non-registration does not lead to invalidation of this charge but merely to the imposition of a fine.[4] By contrast, non-registration of a charge created by a company leads to avoidance of the charge against certain categories of person, notably insolvency practitioners.[5] With this distinction in mind, the decision of the House of Lords in *Abbey National Building Society* v *Cann* [6] is highly significant. In this case a son who had previously received help from his mother in buying a house and in return had been promised by him that she would always have a roof over her head, bought the house with money obtained by means of a mortgage. He subsequently defaulted in payments under the mortgage and the building society sought to repossess the house. The mother and her husband claimed an overriding interest in the house arising by virtue of her occupation in it when the mortgage was created. The House of Lords held that when the son bought with the aid of a mortgage, the acquiring of the legal estate and the granting of the mortgage were one single transaction, that is, there was no *scintilla temporis* during which he held the legal estate free of charge and during which his mother's equitable interest could have attached. As Lord Oliver pointed out:[7]

---

4 S.400 (4), Companies Act 1985.

5 S.395 (1), Companies Act 1985.

6 [1991] 1 AC 56.

7 *Ibid.* at p.92.

> "[T]he acquisition of the legal estate and the charge are not precisely simultaneous but indissolubly bound together . . . the land is, from the very inception, charged with the amount of the loan without which it could never have been transferred at all and it was never intended that it should be otherwise."

As a result of the above approach, the theoretical basis of the seminal judgment of Slade J in *Re Bond Worth* [8] would seem to be undermined. In that case it was held that a clause retaining 'equitable and beneficial ownership' in fibre delivered could only mean that there was a sale of the entire property in the fibre to Bond Worth, which was then followed *eo instanti* by a security being granted to the original supplier by the (now) owner in the form of a chattel mortgage; that is, there was a *scintilla temporis* when Bond Worth became the owner of the fibre. The significance of the House of Lords decision in *Cann* is that it abolishes the *scintilla temporis* doctrine, so that the goods supplied under a retention of title clause are always impressed by the supplier's equitable and beneficial ownership and this is therefore not a charge 'created' by the company.

If full effect were to be given to the decision of the House of Lords in *Cann* then it could be persuasively argued that retention of title clauses which could be categorised as charges could be upheld against insolvency practitioners, for example, in relation to new products made from material sold. However, there are essential differences, not least in terms of commercial context, between a retention of title clause and a conveyance of land in conjunction with a mortgage. The whole purpose of a retention of title clause is to avoid the categorisation of the transaction as being one for security to which the charges regime relates and the relevant consideration is not the *scintilla temporis* doctrine but whether, in relation to the terms of the contract and the circumstances surrounding the contract, a charge has been created in the sense that property has passed to the buyer. This analysis was adopted in *Stroud Architectural Services Ltd* v *John Laing Construction Ltd* [9] where a clause retaining 'equitable and beneficial ownership' in glazing units was construed by John Newey J as a charge created by the buyer. Furthermore it was held that no *scintilla temporis* had occurred in *Bond Worth* since in that case Slade J had referred to the sale and charge back as occurring in *eo instanti*. Admittedly such an approach is a rationalisation and in a sense inductive reasoning,

---

[8] [1980] Ch.28.

[9] [1994] 2 BCLC 276.

but as a matter of principle the general conclusion must be correct, since the commercial reality of (especially) the manufacture of products or their incorporation into finished products with inputs from others must be the creation by the buyer of a charge over what has not become its own finished product. In the context of sale of goods, the source of the security is not exclusively that of the seller as it is, for example, in cases involving mortgages of real estate.

Classifying Retention of Title Clauses

Typically, there are three parts to the reservation of title or '*Romalpa* clause'. The first part is concerned with reserving ownership in the goods themselves. This is satisfactory so long as the buyer remains in possession, but inadequate where, as so often happens, the buyer resells the goods to a third party who when acting in good faith will be protected by virtue of s.25 of the Sale of Goods Act 1979. Hence, the second part of the clause concentrates not on the goods themselves, but the proceeds due to or received by the buyer in the event of resale, and seeks to create a trust in which the original buyer holds these proceeds on behalf of the original seller. The third part of the clause is concerned with the case where the goods having been delivered to the buyer are then used in the process of manufacture, and the device employed here is to declare the finished products as belonging to the seller.

It is appropriate to consider the different ways in which retention of title clauses are framed in order to determine their validity on the basis of legal principle and authority. Broadly speaking, there is the primary clause reserving title to goods *in specie* followed by 'horizontal' extensions into debts; there are also 'vertical' extensions which seek to follow the goods supplied into a finished product or its proceeds.

Simple clauses

The seller retains ownership in the goods delivered as against the buyer until the full purchase price for the goods has been paid. The effectiveness of such a clause has been confirmed in both English and Scots Law and would also appear to be the Irish position.[10] In this respect *Clough Mill* v

---

[10] Many of the important issues in respect of reservation of title clauses are touched upon in the Irish High Court decision in *Re Interview* [1975] IR 382.

Martin,[11] a decision of the Court of Appeal, is the leading English authority. Here the plaintiff supplied yarn to the buyer, a fabric manufacturing company. The contract in question provided that "ownership of the material shall remain with the seller, which reserves the right to dispose of the material until payment in full for all the material has been received by it in accordance with the terms of this contract or until such time as the buyer sells the material to its customers by way of *bona fide* sale at full market value." Following the appointment of the defendant as the receiver to the buyer, the plaintiff sought to recover the unused yarn. The first instance decision that the effect of the clause was to operate as a charge and, therefore, failed for want of registration, was overturned. The validity of the clause was upheld on appeal notwithstanding that it contained a power of re-sale on the part of the buyer.

Current account and money clauses

This is where the seller retains ownership in the goods delivered as against the buyer until all debts or other obligations owed by the buyer to the seller have been paid. The imprimatur here is the House of Lords decision in *Armour* v *Thyssen Edelstahlwerke AG*, [12] a decision on Scots law which upheld the following clause: "All goods delivered by us remain our property (goods remaining in our ownership) until all debts owed to us including any balances existing at relevant times - due to us on any legal grounds - are settled". It was acknowledged by Lord Keith[13] that this clause did 'in a sense give the seller security of title not by virtue of any right over his own property conferred by the buyer'.

On the facts the issue of part payment did not arise, and as a matter of principle the clause is vulnerable for the simple reason that the buyer must be treated as the 'owner' of the goods when he has paid for them, otherwise the clause will be void for total failure of consideration. Whilst it is true that the buyer has received possession and use of the goods, the benefit bargained for is obtaining *property* in the goods which is a pre-condition for their sale as the contract mechanism in this context. Even though the clause can be set aside on the basis of total failure of consideration, this does not mean that the clause has no value in the insolvency context because of the requirement in the Insolvency Rules

---

[11] [1985] 1 WLR 111.

[12] [1991] 2 AC 339.

[13] *Ibid.* p.343.

1987, r 4.90 to set off in liquidation mutual credits, mutual debts or other mutual dealings between the parties. Thus, at the commencement of the winding-up proceedings, the supplier, whilst having to refund the purchase price for total failure of consideration, would have a claim against the buyer for non-payment of other indebtedness and the two claims should be offset against one another.

In Ireland an instructive case in this context is *Frigoscandia Ltd* v *Continental Irish Meat Ltd.*[14] The facts involved the sale of refrigeration equipment subject, *inter alia*, to a current account clause. Following default, the supplier sought to recover the goods on the basis of the retention of title clause. In reaching his conclusion, McWilliam J adopted the classic freedom of contract approach in support of his finding that the parties' intentions, as expressed in the contract should be paramount. He concluded the matter as follows:

> "A difficulty which arises with regard to clauses of this nature is that they are included in the contracts to secure the payment to the vendor of the price of the goods and therefore it may be said as has been argued that the goods once delivered, are intended to be held by the purchaser as security for such payment and that the transaction is in the category of a mortgage in that the vendor, although retaining ownership of an interest in the goods, cannot take possession of them provided that the specified instalments are paid, and that this lead to the conclusion that such a clause must be treated as creating a mortgage or a charge over the goods.
>
> In my opinion such a conclusion can have no general application to these clauses and each case must depend on its own facts. The parties to a contract can agree to any terms they wish, and amongst others, they can agree that the property in the goods shall not pass to the purchaser until all the instalments of the purchase price have been paid."[15]

The prolonged clause

This seeks to reserve title as against the sub-buyer from the original buyer and is likely to be of limited value. The principal reason is not that the clause will amount to a charge, but rather s.25 (1) of the Sale of Goods Act 1979 which provides:-

---

[14] [1982] ILRM 396.

[15] *Ibid.* at p.398.

> "Where a person having bought or agreed to buy goods obtains, with the consent of the seller, possession of the goods or documents of title to the goods, the delivery or transfer by that person, or by a mercantile agent acting for him, of the goods or documents of title, under any sale, pledge, or other disposition thereof, to any person receiving the same in good faith and without notice of any lien or right of the original seller in respect of the goods, has the same effect as if the person making the delivery or transfer were a mercantile agent in possession of the goods or documents of title with the consent of the owner."

Section 25 (1) will not apply where the buyer has bought or agreed to buy goods under a conditional sale agreement regulated by the Consumer Credit Act 1974. It should also be noted that s.25 (1) applies where the person in possession of the goods has acquired them under a contract for the sale of goods. If goods are merely supplied as part of a contract for the provision of work and materials then it will not apply. This is illustrated in *Dawber Williamson Roofing Ltd* v *Humberside County Council* [16] where the plaintiffs agreed to supply and fix roofing slates under a sub-contract with the main contractor subject to a reservation of title clause. The slates were never fixed as the main contractors went into receivership, thereby determining the main and sub-contracts. The defendants had paid the main contractor for the slates through an interim payment and they claimed title by virtue of s.25 (1) Sale of Goods Act 1979. The argument was rejected on the basis that the sub-contract was for the supply and fixing of the roofing materials to which s.25 (1) had no application.

On the assumption that there has been a sale or disposition to the sub-buyer[17] a buyer who has taken possession of goods supplied subject to reservation or title will frequently be able to pass good title to his sub-buyer provided that the latter is in good faith and without notice. A sub-buyer is not put on notice merely because of his knowledge of a retention of title clause not least because there are so many different types. Furthermore, the sub-buyer's knowledge of non-payment cannot be described as bad faith because this can hardly be considered a right "in

---

16 [1979] CLY 212.

17 Compare *Hanson (W) Harrow* v *Rapid Civil Engineering and Usborne Developments* (1987) 38 Build LR 106. The issue becomes acute where in the original sale and also the sub-sale there is a retention of title clause and payment has not been made under either contract. See *Re Highway Foods International Ltd* [1995] BCC 271 where the non-paying sub-buyer could not claim title on the basis of the buyer's own retention of title clause.

respect of goods"; it is merely a personal right in respect of the contract of sale.

Proceeds clauses

This extends a retention of title clause to the proceeds of resale of the goods supplied. As an equitable tracing right which arises by operation of law this is not registrable as a charge since such a right has not been conferred or created by the debtor company. Furthermore, if the traceable funds are mixed then equity may declare a charge on the mixed fund. The point of principle is whether a fiduciary relationship can be established in relation to the proceeds, which of course depends upon the categorisation of the relationship as one of principal and agent. In England, the general approach has been hostile to such clauses and there has been a reluctance to find for a fiduciary relationship, even where the obligee is under an obligation to separate the proceeds of sales from other moneys and pass on all the rights relating to the sub-sales to the seller. Thus, in *Tatung (UK) Ltd* v *Galex Telesure Ltd*,[18] Phillips J found that despite elaborate contractual provision having been made which effectively fettered the obligee's ability to deal with the proceeds, nevertheless this was categorised as a charge on the basis that the source of the plaintiff's rights was the contract and not equitable principles arising by operation of law. Such an approach does seem odd because it is tantamount to penalising the suppliers for being over-specific which would, if anything, suggest that they were acting as owners in relation to the process - it might have been thought that the fiduciary relationship argument would have been strengthened by these provisions in the contract.[19]

A more recent English case tends to confirm the hostility of the English courts to proceeds clauses, because in *Modelboard Ltd* v *Outer Box Ltd*,[20] Hart QC sitting as a Deputy High Court judge, held that a clause which provided that the buyers were held 'in trust for the [seller]' was by way of charge. The judge was concerned by the apparent commercial consequences of upholding a proceeds clause, namely, had the buyer resold at a profit then the commercial sense of the arrangement had to be that the supplier after satisfying the outstanding indebtedness would be obliged to account to the buyer for the balance. However, this conclusion need not

18 (1989) 5 BCC 325.

19 See also *Compaq Computer Ltd* v *Abercorn Group Ltd* [1993] BCLC 602.

20 [1993] BCLC 623.

follow where the obligee is categorised as a commission agent, since the profit margin could be treated by the seller and the buyer as the buyer's agency commission. In large measure, this argument draws upon the approach of Jessel MR in *Re Smith, ex p Bright* who held:[21]

> "There is nothing to prevent the principal from remunerating the agent by a commission varying according to the amount of the profit obtained by the sale. *A fortiori* there is nothing to prevent his paying a commission depending upon the surplus which the agent can obtain over and above the price which will satisfy the principal . . ."

The commission agency arrangement in the *Romalpa* context would be seriously compromised if it fell within the terms of the Commercial Agents (Council Directive) Regulations 1993.[22] This provides agents who sell by commission with levels of job security and compensation for loss of office comparable to those enjoyed by employees. In addition it imposes obligations upon principals as to payment of commission and also as to compensation at the end of the agency agreement. Such obligations do not reflect the commercial reality in a proceeds clause, and it is noteworthy that the Regulations do not apply to commercial agents dealing with property on their own account. In this respect, the analysis of the arrangement is crucial: there is nothing inconsistent between a proceeds clause and a contract for the sale of goods, because s.25 (1) of the Sale of Goods Act 1979 provides that a buyer may 'agree to buy goods' and still pass a good title to a purchaser in good faith and without notice. Moreover, a commission agent does not establish privity between his principal and a third party and this internal agency arrangement is at the heart of Roskill LJ's judgment in *Romalpa*, that is, under the head sale, the seller and buyer could stand in any agency relationship but as between buyer and sub-buyers the buyer sold as a principal:

> "I see no difficulty in the contractual concept that, as between the defendants and their sub-purchasers, the defendants sold as principals, but that, as between themselves and the plaintiffs, those goods which they were selling as principals within their implied authority from the plaintiffs' view were the plaintiffs' goods which they were selling as agents for the plaintiffs to whom they remained fully accountable." [23]

---

[21] (1879) 10 Ch App 566 at p.570.

[22] SI 1993 No.3053.

[23] *Loc cit* fn.1 at p.690.

This view appears to be supported by the Court of Appeal decision in *Welsh Development Agency* v *Export Finance Co Ltd.*[24]

Considerable complexity of drafting may be necessary in the hope that the clause may ultimately attract judicial sympathy. Thus in drafting such a clause the buyer/agent should be subject to an obligation to keep the proceeds of sale in a separate bank account and to account to the seller for them, at least to the extent of the original sale price. Of course the commercial reality of everyday business has to be accommodated and such requirement may prove unacceptable or unworkable to the buyer as a matter of commercial practice. In Scotland, proceeds of sale clauses face additional difficulties not encountered under English law. Under Scots Trust law, where the truster and trustee are the same person (as they would be in the case of a buyer receiving proceeds of sale under a sub-sale) for an express trust to be validly constituted there must be a trust asset in existence and there must also be delivery of the trust deed in order to achieve the irrevocable divestiture of the truster and investiture of the trustee in the trust estate.[25] Obvious difficulties arise in a *Romalpa* context since, at the time of sale of the goods by the original seller, in most cases, there will be no existing trust funds. The buyer will not, at that stage, normally have received the proceeds of any sub-sale. Indeed, he may not even have entered into a sub-sale. It has been suggested that a constructive trust might arise in favour of the owner of goods where the buyer from him sells goods without himself having acquired title. As yet, this idea is untested in the courts but, in any event, there remains the difficulty of identifying the trust property. Alternatively, it seems that the concept of agency might be employed in order to create a fiduciary relationship between the buyer and seller so that sub-sale proceeds are held subject to a constructive trust for the seller. As under English law, any proceeds of sale clause should require the proceeds to be kept separate from other funds belonging to the buyer. Provided that obligation is observed, the tracing of those funds will be possible under Scots law. Even where the buyer mixes trust funds with his own, the law will still allow the trust funds to be traced. If the trustee draws funds from a mixed account he will be considered to withdraw his own funds first rather than those of the trust

---

24 [1992] BCLC 148.

25 *Clark Taylor and Co Ltd* v *Quality Site Development (Edinburgh) Ltd* [1981] SC 111. An earlier case, *Export Credits Guarantee Department* v *Turner* [1979] SC 286, also held that the declaration of the trust fund is invalid if the trust property was not possessed by the trustor at that time.

estate.[26] The tracing rules are not consistent and reference should be made to specialist texts in this regard.

The possibility of a retention of title clause constituting a charge over book debts was considered by Phillips J in *E Pfeiffer Weinkellerei-Weineinkauf GmbH and Co* v *Arbuthnot Factors Ltd.*[27] In the *Arbuthnot Factors* case, the contract between the plaintiff supplier and Springfield Wine Importers Ltd set out comprehensively the nature of the interest which the plaintiff was to have by way of security in respect of debts created by sub-sales. The retention of title clause was (translated from the original German) as follows:

> "All claims that [the importer] gets from the sale . . . with all rights including his profit amounting to his obligations towards [Pfeiffer], will be passed on to [Pfeiffer]. On demand the [importer] is obliged to notify the assignment of the claim to give [Pfeiffer] in writing all necessary information concerning the assertion of [Pfieffer's] claims . . . In case of cash sales, the money that has come from a third person immediately becomes [Pfeiffer's] . . . this money has to be separated from other money, it must be booked correspondingly, and must be administered until called for."

Springfield had agreed to assign to the plaintiff the future debts owed by the sub-purchasers to Springfield up to the amount of Springfield's outstanding indebtedness to the plaintiff. Subsequently, Springfield then entered into a factoring agreement with the defendant which amounted to an assignment of the future debts.

The approach taken by Phillips J is interesting in that he held that Springfield was not a bailee or any kind of fiduciary with respect to the plaintiff, and he found that the *Romalpa* case went the way it did because of the defendant's concession that it was a bailee of the plantiff's goods. The normal implication, Phillips J considered, is that a buyer in possession, to whom title has not yet passed, when permitted to sub-sell in the ordinary course of his business does so for his own account. Such an approach is too extensive. The main objection against an agency relation is that the dealer is permitted to keep the profits on sub-sale. In *Bond Worth*,[28] Slade J cited *Re Nevill ex p White*[29] as authority for this proposition.

---

26 *Jopp* v *Johnston's Trustee* [1904] 6 F 1028.

27 [1988] 1 WLR 150.

28 *Loc cit* fn. 8.

29 (1871) 6 Ch App 397.

Nonetheless, it is important to recognise that the court in *Ex p White* was concerned with the substance of the relationship between the supplier and dealer. The court considered that, on the facts, the two-month credit period, together with the fact that the dealer was under no duty to account and could sell for whatever price he wished, pointed to a debtor-creditor relationship. Neither should a credit period count against beneficial ownership of the proceeds; the credit allows the dealer to extend a similar period of credit to a subsequent purchaser, although the dealer will have to account as soon as the proceeds are in fact received.

In contrast to the approach taken in the *Arbuthnot Factors* case, in the Irish case of *SA Foundaries du Lion MV International Factors (Ireland) Ltd*,[30] the court found (Barrington J presiding) that the plaintiff supplier had a valid proceeds clause which prevailed over the defendant's factoring arrangement. The Irish cases are not consistent in this regard as seen, for example, in the Irish High Court decision of *Carroll Group Distributors Ltd* v *G and JF Bourke Ltd and Bourke Sales Ltd*.[31] In this case the retention of title clause provided that the property in the goods should remain in the plaintiff until the defendants had discharged all sums, but gave the defendants an express right to resell the goods. The clause further provided that, following resale, the defendants undertook to hold moneys received "in trust" for the plaintiff and to maintain an independent account of all sums received. It was held by Murphy J that the arrangement was in substance a charge on the proceeds of sub-sale because:

> ". . . the bargain made between the parties . . . properly implemented would result in a bank account with sums of money credited thereto which would probably be in excess of the amounts due by [the defendants] to [the plaintiff]. This would arise partly from the fact that the proceeds of sale would include some goods the cost price of which had been discharged and some had not. In other words the bank account would be a fund to which [the plaintiffs] could have recourse to ensure the discharge of the money due to them even though they would not be entitled to the entirety of that fund. Accordingly the fund agreed to be credited would possess all the characteristics of a mortgage or charge as identified by Romer LJ in *In Re George Inglefield Ltd* [1933] Ch.1 at 27-28."[32]

---

30 [1983] ILRM 66.

31 [1990] ILRM 285.

32 *Ibid*. at p.289.

An important aspect of Phillips J's judgment in *Arbuthnot Factors* is the conclusion that a charge, by virtue of the proceeds clause, had been created over the book debt which required registration under s.395 of the Companies Act 1985. Of considerable commercial significance is the possibility of a fixed charge on book debts but in order to achieve this the company creating the charge must be limited in the manner in which it can deal with the debts.[33] In many instances the elaborate and restrictive provisions concerning the collection of the debts necessarily consequent on a fixed charge are not going to be commercially acceptable.

Aggregation clauses

For the sake of convenience, discussion of the aggregation clause will be split into the categories identified below:

(i) Where a new product is created whether wholly or partly from the supplier's goods in circumstances where there is a loss of identity of the supplier's goods (specificatio). The obvious policy dilemma here is that of windfall, because the supplier would recover not only the buyer's processing efforts but also any new materials supported by third parties. Indeed, these considerations were alluded to by Robert Goff LJ in *Clough Mill* when he said:[34]

> "Now it is no doubt true that, where A's material is lawfully used by B to create new goods, whether or not B incorporated other material of his own, property in the new goods will generally rest in B, at least where the goods are not reducible to the original materials (see *Blackstone Commentaries* (17th ed; 1830, vol.2, pp.404-405)."

---

33 The principal authority in Ireland is *Re Keenan Bros Ltd* [1986] BCLC 242 whereas in England the seminal decision is *Siebe Gorman and Co Ltd* v *Barclays Bank Ltd* [1979] 2 Lloyd's Rep 142. For an authoritative discussion see Gough *Company Charges* (Butterworth) 2nd ed (1996) pp.609-630. See *Re Cosslett (Contractors) Ltd* [1997] BCC 724; *re BCCI (No.8)* [1998] AC 214. A distinction is drawn between debt and proceeds so it has been held in *re New Bullas Trading* [1994] BCC 36 that a direction to pay proceeds into an account plus minimal restrictions will create a fixed charge. Compare *re Westmaze Ltd* (May 15, 1998); re *Double S Printers Ltd* (March 25, 1998).

34 *Loc. cit* fn.11 at p.119.

Parties cannot by their contractual stipulations alone alter the application of the principles and rules of the law of property. It follows that if the supplier qualifies his interest in the finished product in order to avoid an unintentioned windfall for himself, this is tantamount to a security for the debt, that is, the arrangement will be categorised as creating a charge over the new goods. Nevertheless as Robert Goff LJ went on to point out in *Clough Mill*, it is possible for the parties to agree that title should pass in the new goods to the supplier under a retention of title clause. What is clear is that without any express provision, a supplier will lose title to his goods once the manufacture process commences.[35]

In Scotland, though not a case involving reservation of title as such, *The International Banking Corporation & Ors* v *Ferguson, Shaw & Sons*[36] confirms that, under the doctrine of *specificatio*, title will be lost by a supplier where his goods are irreversibly turned into other products. The owner of a quantity of oil, which had subsequently been made into lard, enjoyed no title to the lard. Even where specific provision has been made in relation to the title of the new products, the courts have not so far looked favourably upon them. *Re Peachdart Ltd*[37] suggests that title will be lost once the goods undergo processing notwithstanding that they may not be mixed with other products to any substantial degree. Here leather was supplied for the purpose of handbag manufacture. The relevant clause in the sale contract stated that "if any of the products are incorporated in or used a material for other goods before . . . payment the property in the whole of such other goods shall be and remain with the seller until such payment has been made". The clause also required the buyer to act in a fiduciary capacity and permitted the seller to trace the proceeds of sale. It was held that once the leather had been appropriated into the handbag making process, the effect of the clause was such that the seller lost title to the leather and instead held a charge over the proceeds of sale of both completed and uncompleted handbags. Since that charge had not been registered, it was void. *Re Peachdart* was decided before Goff LJ's comments in *Clough Mill*. In that case the "simple" element of the retention of title clause in question was upheld but a further sub-section which purported to give the original seller title to any new product was considered to amount to a charge. This appears to have been partly

---

35 See *Borden (U K.) Ltd* v *Scottish Timber Products Ltd* [1981] Ch 25.

36 [1910] SC182.

37 [1984] Ch 131.

because it would give the seller a windfall profit in relation to those new products and also because of the possibility that the seller's goods may have been mixed with goods supplied by other third parties (as opposed to goods belonging just to the buyer).

In summary, the Courts seem reluctant to construe a clause giving title to a supplier in products manufactured from his original goods and those of the buyer. It also appears clear that where the goods of two third parties are combined in the manufacturing process, a retention of title clause purporting to accord title in the new goods to one of those suppliers will amount to a charge. This approach was confirmed in *Chaigley Farms Ltd* v *Crawford, Kaye and Grayshire Ltd* [38] where it was held that the identity of livestock was changed once it had been slaughtered by the buyer and the slaughtered animal could no longer be described as "livestock" under the retention of title clause.

(ii) Where there is a mixture of the supplier's products with those of another ("confusio" or "commixtio"). Generally speaking, where the goods of different owners are mixed without the physical characteristics of the goods being affected, the owners of the original goods will become co-owners as tenants in common of the admixture in proportion to their contribution to that admixture.[39] Likewise, in Scotland, the several owners will become *pro indiviso* owners of the mixed products according to the proportion of their original shares. Such co-ownership arises by operation of law. Accordingly an express charge which merely reflects this principle, should not amount to a registrable charge. In England, s.10 of the Torts (Interference with Goods) Act 1977 may be of some assistance to a supplier. It states that co-ownership is not a defence to an action founded on conversion or trespass to goods where the defendant, without the authority of the co-owner either:-

---

[38] [1996] BCC 957. Compare the position in New Zealand where it was held that logs retained their identity despite being cut into planks. See *Pongakawa Sawmill Ltd* v *New Zealand Forest Products Ltd* [1992] 3 NZLR 304.

[39] *Indian Oil Corporation Ltd* v *Greenstone Shipping SA (Panama)* [1998] 1 QB 345. In *Forsythe International (UK) Ltd* v *Silver Shipping Co Ltd* [1994] 1 WLR 1334, it was accepted by the parties that a retention of title clause was still valid in respect of oil bunkers against a charterparty purchasing the fuel even though it must have been mixed with other fuel on board the ship.

"(a) destroys the goods or disposes of the goods in a way giving a good title to the entire property in the goods, or otherwise does anything equivalent to destruction of the other's interest in the goods, or

(b) purports to dispose of the goods in a way which would give a good title to the entire property in the goods if he was acting with the authority of all co-owners of the goods."

(iii) Where there is accession of property belonging to one person to the property of another (accessio or *adjuncto).* In both England and Scotland, the general rule is that the owner of the principal goods will acquire title to any accessions made to those principal goods. Whether there has been accession will depend on the degree of annexation. In the retention of title context, the difficulty that arises is that, in the case of an express clause, the supplier is arguably attempting to acquire title to goods which were not originally his in order to secure payment of the purchase price. Accordingly, a clause purporting to vest ownership of such accessories to the supplier may amount to a charge. However, if the accession merely arises by operation of the doctrine of accession, it is arguable that a charge has not been created since ownership to the accessory vests in the owner of the dominant property by operation of law.

The principles of accession have not been the subject of extensive judicial comment in the context of *Romalpa* clauses but were considered in *Hendy Lennox (Industrial Engines) Ltd* v *Grahame Puttick Ltd.*[40] Diesel engines had been supplied for incorporation into generating sets. The supplier retained title to the engines notwithstanding such incorporation because the degree of annexation was held to be not sufficient for the engines to have acceded to the generators.

Repossession of the goods

From a practical point of view, if a supplier of goods is to be able to recover goods from his customer in the event of non-payment or insolvency, he will need the right to enter the buyer's premises and, once there, find his goods. Retention of title clauses should provide expressly that the seller is authorised to enter the buyer's premises and re-possess the goods. Without such a clause, or other permission from the buyer, the seller will be unable to enter the premises without committing a trespass. Even with the benefit of such clause, the seller may still find access is

40 [1984] 1 WLR 485.

denied. In such circumstances, forcible entry will be possible only with the authority of a court order. Further, the clause should specifically provide for separate storage or separate identification of the seller's goods. This is advisable partly because it may provide evidence of the fiduciary nature or the relationship. Practically, it also allows the goods to be found more easily once entry had been made. The obligation may also usefully be coupled with a right of entry enabling the seller to inspect the premises on occasion to ensure that the buyer's duty to maintain separate storage is being observed. A clause stipulating a right of re-entry does not operate as a land charge for the purposes of English land law.

If an administrative receiver refuses the supplier access, the latter in an attempt to secure this can ask the High Court to grant him an *Anton Piller* Order [41] which will have to be done quickly if it is to have any effect at all. Nevertheless, the costs associated with this may be prohibitive especially when coupled by the fact that the supplier cannot be sure of recovering the costs of the application from the administrative receiver, and there is no guarantee anyway that the goods are still on the premises.

Retention of Title Clauses and Insolvency

The 1986 Insolvency Act envisages the appointment of an administrator as an interim step to save a business. Consistent with this goal, no steps can be taken to enforce a retention of title clause without the consent of either the court or the administrator.[42] The latter is given the power to dispose of property subject to a retention of title clause so long as one or more of the purposes specified in the administrative order is satisfied. The administrative receiver will have to notify all known creditors of the company under s.21 (*b*) of the Insolvency Act 1986, presumably advising them of his appointment and any claim they may have, for example, by way of set-off or retention of title clause. Significantly under s.234 (4) of the Insolvency Act 1986, personal liability is removed if the administrator, administrative receiver or liquidator *reasonably* believes and is not negligent that the goods belong to the insolvent company. Under this scenario, fault must be proven and this requires a higher standard of proof than that required for conversion, as seen in *Clough Mill* v *Martin*.[43] The

---

[41] *Anton Piller KG* v *Manufacturing Processes Ltd* [1976] Ch 55.

[42] S.10 (1), Insolvency Act 1986.

[43] *Loc. cit.* fn.11. See *Vale Sewing Machines* v *Robb* [1997] SCLR 797.

supplier is in an invidious position because he will have to prove that his goods were on the premises at the time of the receivership. Moreover, even if the administrator or administrative receiver disposes of the goods negligently, s.234 (4) (*b*) of the 1986 Act anticipates that he can retain a lien on the proceeds of disposal for his own expenses.

Neither the White Paper[44] nor the 1985 and 1986 Insolvency Acts gave a discussion on reservation of title clauses, presumably because the approach of the Cork Committee on Insolvency Proceedings[45] was deemed to resolve the matter. The Cork Committee recommended a moratorium of 12 months from the commencement of a receivership with regard to the benefit of enforcing a reservation of title clause.[46] Although bankruptcy proceedings promote the collective will, it is doubtful whether the repossession of collateral by the secured creditor should interfere with this bankruptcy goal, since if the secured party's collateral is worth more to the firm than to the third party, that collateral should end up back in the hands of the firm notwithstanding its repossession by the secured creditor in the interim. In practice though, there is no doubt that such repossession would hinder efforts to preserve the firm as a 'going concern', and there may be substantial costs involved in repossession and the subsequent repurchase. One way of balancing the tensions here is to substitute for a secured party actual substantive *rights*, a requirement that the secured creditor accept the equivalent *value* of those rights. There is nothing anomalous in this approach because if the firm is worth more as a going concern than if it is broken up, giving the secured creditor the benefit of his bargain should not prevent a firm from staying together. Indeed, a failure to recognise the secured creditor's rights in full would prejudice the bankruptcy goal of ensuring that the assets are used to advance the interest of everyone.

The above considerations are reflected in ss.10 (1) and 11 (3) of the Insolvency Act 1986. These sections provide for a statutory freeze procedure on the enforcement of real and personal rights against the company pending the hearing of a petition for an administration order and during the currency of any order that is made. The implication here is that there is nothing to prevent the seller terminating the agreement, but he cannot repossess the goods. This stems from the role of the administrator as the official corporate rescuer. One way of avoiding this conclusion is to

---

44 *A Revised Framework for Insolvency Law* (Cmnd. 9175, 1984).

45 *Insolvency Law and Practice* (Cmnd. 8558, 1982).

46 *Ibid* at para. 1650.

provide in the contract of sale that payment should be made by the buyer not to the seller but to an associated company; in this way it would not come within the definition of a retention of title clause under s.251 of the Insolvency Act 1986, which anticipates a stipulation for payment to the seller. It is worth noting that Pt II of the Insolvency Act 1986 does not extinguish entitlements; it merely restricts enforcement to a substantial extent while the order remains in force. This was emphasised in the Practice Guidelines (Insolvency Administration) issued by the Court of Appeal following its decision in *Re Atlantic Computers*.[47] Leave to object to the moratorium sought by the administrator may be granted where it would cause significant loss to the applicant.[48] In its assessment of this, the court would have regard to such matters as the company's financial position, the administrator's proposals, the period during which the administration order had been in force and was expected to remain in force, the effect on the administration if leave were given and upon the applicant if it were refused and lastly, the end result sought to be achieved by the administration with the prospects of it being achieved. However, at the same time s.27 of the 1986 Act provides that any creditor or member can apply to the court for relief on the grounds that the company's affairs, business or property are being, or will be, managed by the administrator in a manner unfairly prejudicial to the interest of some part of the members of creditors. In this event, the court may under s.27 (4) discharge the administration order. Thus it would appear prudent for the administrator, when using the goods, to pay at least the use value of the goods. This action will prevent an application to the court by the seller on the ground of prejudice under s.27 of the Insolvency Act 1986. Even so in *Re Charnley Davies Ltd (No 2)* [49] it was held that a sale at a negligent undervalue was not sufficient without more to establish a claim for relief under s.27. In this respect Millet J held that whilst professional negligence would amount to misconduct this would not necessarily evidence unfairly prejudicial management in the light of the need to have proper regard for the interest of all the creditors.

---

[47] [1992] Ch 505.

[48] The moratorium does not alter or destroy these rights and the judgment of the administrator in refusing leave to the owner of goods to retake them may be reviewed by the Court. See *Barclays Mercantile Business Finance Ltd* v *SIBEC Developments Ltd* [1992] 1 WLR 1253.

[49] [1990] BCLC 760.

One of the most important features of the Insolvency Act 1986 is s.15. What is anticipated here is that the administrator can dispose of the goods in the company's possession which are held on retention of title as if they were unencumbered by the company. This is achieved by applying for a court order to authorise disposal, and the court in making the order has to be satisfied that one or more of the purposes specified in the administration order will be satisfied. The purposes for which the order can be made are found in s.8. In this event, suppliers of goods under effective retention of title clauses will receive either the net proceeds of the sale, or if they are determined by the court to be less than the market value of the goods, sums will be provided to make up the market value by virtue of s.15 (5) (*b*). Nevertheless, there are important limitations here. First, the court is under no obligation to view invoice value at the time of supply as 'market value' at the time of disposal. Secondly, there is no mechanism by which a supplier of goods on retention of title can object to disposal. In contrast, in the case of administrative receivership, although s.43 of the Act gives similar powers to those enjoyed by the administrator it would seem that retention of title clauses are excluded. This is because s.43 refers to the disposal of property which is subject to 'security' and this is defined as 'any mortgage, charge, lien or other security'.[50] Following on from this, it would seem that the validity of a retention of title clause has still to be determined. Thus, if the administrative receiver disputes the validity of the claim, the price of the goods will be paid into a joint deposit account, a practice which exactly mirrors the position of receiverships before the advent of the 1986 Act.

It is interesting that the approach taken under the 1986 Act concentrates upon economic substance rather than legal form. Consequently, the moratorium provisions discussed above extend to hire purchase agreement, chattel leasing arrangement (bailment of goods capable of subsisting for more than three months) and a retention of title clause. Strangely, the definition proffered for retention of title clause would have extended to all three credit instruments, namely an agreement for the sale of goods which does not constitute a charge on the goods but under which, if the seller is not paid and the company is wound up, the seller will have priority over all other creditors as respects the goods or any property representing the goods.[51] Here we find echoes of the accountant's

---

[50] S. 248 (*b*), Insolvency Act 1986.

[51] S. 251, Insolvency Act 1986.

approach to retention of title clauses. Soon after the *Romalpa* decision (1976), the Institute of Chartered Accountants in England and Wales recommended that the commercial reality of the situation should be accommodated in the accounts, that is, it should be treated as a sale since this is the intention of both buyer and seller.[52] The position is that provided a business shows all the signs of remaining a 'going concern', the sale of goods subject to reservation of title should be treated in the accounts of both the buyer and the seller in the same manner as an outright sale.

Private International Law Considerations

The simple clause

The validity of a retention of title clause as between seller and buyer should be determined by the *lex situs* of the goods at the time they are despatched to the buyer. Some authorities suggest that the proper law of the contract of sale should determine whether the property has passed and this is justified on the basis that it reflects the parties' intention.[53] This approach is difficult to support and the general principal is that the rules relating to the passing of title are governed by the *lex situs* of the goods or the products made out of them, at the time of sub-sale. In very many instances the law of the contract and the *lex situs* will be the same, so the validity of the retention of title clause should not prove to be problematical in this respect. Where the proper law is not the same as the *lex situs*, conflicts may arise, but the *lex situs* should prevail.[54] Nonetheless, Sheriff Jardine in the Scottish case of *Hammer and Sohne* v *HWT Realisation Ltd* [55] arrived at a different conclusion which is worthy of further discussion.

In *Hammer* the facts revolved around the validity of an "all sums due" retention of title clause in a contract between a German firm (the plaintiffs)

---

[52] Institute of Chartered Accountants in England and Wales, Statement V24, now Statement 2: 207.

[53] Compare *Badische Anilin und Soda Fabrık* v *Basle Chemical Works Bindschedler* [1898] AC 200; *Kursell* v *Timber Operators and Contractors Ltd* [1927] 1 KB 299.

[54] *Re Interview* [1975] IR 382; *Kruppstahl* v *Quıtmann Products Ltd* [1982] ILRM 351.

[55] [1985] SLT 21.

and a Scottish firm (the defendants). The defendants were in receivership and the plaintiffs asked the Sheriff for an order for delivery of certain items of jewellery (located in Scotland) which accounted for the balance owed to them. The clause stated *inter alia*, "Ownership shall not be transferred to the buyer until he has redeemed all liabilities . . . arising from his business connection with us". Under German law, the proper law of the contract, the clause was valid, but in Scottish law its validity was prone to attack on the basis that it attempted to create a non-possessory security interest. In *Hammer*, Sheriff Jardine applied Scots law as the *lex situs* maintaining that "the effectiveness or otherwise of the security falls to be determined by the law of the place where the goods in question are actually located".[56] Had the contract been categorised as one of *sale of goods*, rather than as creating a security interest, the *lex situs* of the contract would suggest the law of the country where the goods were situated when the contract was formed should have been applied. Even so, the decision in the case could have been justified on the basis that although a valid security interest had been created in German law as the *lex situs*, it would not be recognised in Scotland on the basis of public policy. This appears to have been the approach adopted by Lord Davidson in *Zahnrad Fabrik Passau GmbH* v *Terex Ltd*[57] when he stated that:

> " . . . in a contract regulating the rights and obligations . . . of two contracting parties, *prima facie* I see no reason why they should not incorporate into the contract one or more provision of a foreign legal system. If the contracting parties choose to do that, then the condition relied upon may be open to challenge on . . . the ground that is opposed to a fundamental principle of the law of Scotland."[58]

Proceeds clauses

In international transactions where there is a duty to account for proceeds, the following questions inevitably arise: First, what is the relevant law by which the obligation to account is determined? Second, what law governs the proper remedy by which the obligation to account, if it exists under the appropriate law, is to be enforced? As a matter of strict logic, the validity of the proceeds clause should be governed by the proper law of the sale

---

[56] *Ibid.* p.23.
[57] [1986] SLT 84.
[58] *Ibid* at p.88.

contract since this presumably reflects the parties' intention. Of course, it may be that such a clause will be struck down if the proper law construes it as a charge. This is demonstrated in Lord Mayfield's approach in the Scottish Court of Session in *Armour and Another* v *Thyssen Edelstahlwerke AG.*[59] In this case, the pursuers were joint receivers of a Scottish manufacturing company whilst the defenders were German steel suppliers. The defenders delivered steel to the pursuers before the receivership and before they received payment. The contract between the parties included *inter alia* a provision reserving to the vendor title in goods delivered to the purchaser until payment of all debts due to the vendor by the purchaser had been satisfied. As a matter of fact, it was found that the defenders had not displaced the onus on them to prove that under German law the clause was a simple reservation of title clause. In any case, Lord Mayfield considered that what was involved here was the creation of a real right so that the *lex situs* to be applied was that of the place where the goods were actually located, that is, Scotland. The suggestions that the law of (West) Germany should be applied as the *lex situs*, that being the place where the goods were located at the time of the formation of the contract, was rejected. The categorisation of the clause as constituting a security device compromised the determination of the *lex situs*. The better approach would have been to consider the contract as one of sale, the *lex situs* of the contract being the law of the country where the goods are situated when the contract is formed. This question was not considered by the House of Lords. Nonetheless, their lordships restated the conventional legal position accepted by the Court of Appeal in England that there was an effective reservation of title clause sanctioned by ss.17 and 19 Sale of Goods Act 1979 and, as such, this did not constitute an invalid security interest.

Significant problems arise as to which law governs the enforcement of the obligation to account. Where the recognition of the foreign remedy would cause an English court undue inconvenience because of, for example, the absence of procedural machinery for enforcement, the English court could then be justified in applying the corresponding English remedy. A closely related problem is that where a sub-purchaser has not acquired a good title to the goods under the appropriate *lex situs*, and the original seller may have an action for wrongful interference against the sub-buyer. If this interference has occurred abroad, the English rules for

[59] [1986] SLT 452.

the choice of law in tort will apply. These rules require that the interference be wrongful under English law and also actionable according to the law of the place where the interference took place.

Extended clauses

Where the clause purports to vest in the seller title to manufacturer goods incorporating raw materials supplied by the seller, the validity of the clause will be determined by the laws of the country where the manufactured product is produced, that being the relevant *lex situs*. Thus in the *Armour* case, the pursuers (joint receivers) claimed a certain amount of the steel on the basis of specification (the creation of a new thing). This claim was upheld by Lord Mayfield in the Scottish Court of Session because the steel had been cut and was thereby usable only in limited circumstances. The *lex situs* was Scottish law.

In certain circumstances the proper law of the contract will be relevant. This is illustrated in the case of *Zahnrad Fabrik Passau GmbH* v *Terex Ltd.* [60] The facts involved a supply by a German company (Zahnrad) of vehicle components which were sold and delivered to the defenders, a Scottish company, before the appointment of a receiver. The German company sought to rely upon its retention of title clause which it alleged had been incorporated into the main conditions of supply. This clause provided *inter alia* for a retention of ownership or part ownership if the goods should form integral parts of a further individual object. Lord Davidson held *obiter* that if a Scottish buyer was able to show accession by the criteria set down under Scots law[61] then it would be possible for the pursuers to rely on their contractual term involving a more rigorous test of accession to defeat that claim. He agreed that on the question of accession, the difference between German law and Scots law was not fundamental, especially in view of the fact that s.17 Sale of Goods Act 1979 makes property passing an aspect of contract. At first sight, it is difficult to understand this argument because s.17 refers only to the transfer of ownership of goods on *sale*, and accession can hardly be said to constitute this. Nonetheless, it could be argued, the parties to a contract may determine if and when accession might take place in Scots law and in whom the property vests: if this is so, there is no reason why the Scots *lex*

---

60 *Loc. cit.* fn.57.

61 *Wylie and Lockhead* v *Mitchell* (1970) 8 M 552.

situs may not refer this question to another legal system, probably the proper law of the contract.

In large measure, the dilemmas posed by more extended retention of title clauses reflect commercial reality; thus, elements of both contract and conveyance are included in such clauses. This can easily be demonstrated in the case of a proceeds clause which seeks to enable the original seller to maintain a *direct* action against sub-purchasers for the sub-sale price of the goods. The law here is obscure. If this assignment of debt is treated as an aspect of contract, its validity will depend upon the proper law of the sub-sale which governs the debt. Nonetheless, the better view, it is submitted, is that since the assignment of a debt involves a proprietary right, the question of whether the debt is capable of assignment should be determined according to the *lex situs*, namely the law of the place where the debtor resides, as this will represent the *situs* of the debt.

Registration of charges

The issue of the need or otherwise to register a retention of title clause as a security interest under the Companies Act 1985 will be determined according to English law.[62] In *Re Interview*,[63] Kenny J found that the supply contracts were governed by German law which recognised the current account type of reservation of title agreement, but the assignment of debts arising from sub-sales constituted a charge on the book debts and required registration under s.99(2)(*c*) Irish Companies Act 1963. The Irish High Court decision (Gannon J presiding) in *Kruppstahl AG* v *Quitmann Products Ltd* [64] is instructive and is worthy of further consideration. The facts revolved around a contract to supply steel between German plaintiff suppliers and the Irish defendants. The contract was expressed to be subject to German law and included *inter alia* the following provision:

> "In the case of processing, blending and mixing of the reserved goods with other goods by the buyer, we acquire a joint title to the new goods in accordance with the ratio of the invoice value of the reserved goods to the invoice value of the other goods used. If our title lapses due to blending or mixing, the buyer assigns to us already at this stage his title to the new goods

---

[62] *Re Weldtech Equipment Ltd* [1991] BCC 16.

[63] *Loc. cit.* fn.54.

[64] [1982] ILRN 551.

in accordance with the invoice value of the reserved goods, and holds them in trust for us, without charge."

Following the receivership of the defendants, the plaintiffs sought to exercise their rights under the contract of sale. As far as manufactured steel incorporating metal supplied by the plaintiffs was concerned, Gannon J held that the seller could have no proprietary interest because the clause amounted to a registrable charge. The *nature* of the charge created under s.99 Companies Act 1963 (the Irish equivalent of s.395 English Companies Act (1985)) was never clearly established. The clause expressly provided for joint ownership and for tenancy in common. As such, the clause could be construed as not requiring registration. Nonetheless, Gannon J was impressed by the fact that the possessor of the goods was allowed to sell them and recover the value of his workmanship. This interest had been assigned in advance under the contract to the seller so that Gannon J concluded: "Any such assignment can be construed only as an equitable interest in the nature of a floating charge".[65]

Drafting Considerations with Retention of Title Clauses

There exists a fine line between what is commercially acceptable and what is legally necessary in order to ensure priority. A retention of title clause, if it is not to be attacked on the basis of sham should provide the following:

(1) The possessor of the goods should be described as a commission agent in the case where resale of goods *in specie* is anticipated. Where this is not the case, the possessor should be described as a fiduciary bailee and agent.

(2) On resale, the commission agent should be described as selling as principal.

(3) There should be an express obligation to account for all proceeds relating to the goods supplied, including insurance proceeds. Moreover, there should be included an obligation to keep the proceeds separate and identifiable.

(4) There should be an obligation to store the goods supplied in a proper fashion and that warehousing arrangements should ensure that the goods are identifiable. Risk should be described as having passed whilst an obligation to insure should at the same time be imposed.

---

[65] *Ibid* at p.560.

Ancillary rights should also be incorporated, for example, a right of access to ensure against the charge of trespass. Such a right of entry should be associated with specific contractual contingencies, the most important being non-payment. Additionally, there should be a provision giving the supplier a right of removal.

(5) In the case of fungible goods which are mixed with others, tenancy in common provision should be incorporated.

(6) Where the possessor works through the application of labour or commingling in relation to the goods supplied, in order to avoid the possibility of a registrable charge, the nature of the relationship should be described in bailment for commodity processing terms.

Conclusion

An enforceable retention of title clause is a useful tool for a supplier of goods to include in his sale contract. Properly worded simple or all monies clauses should accord him a priority over other creditors in the event of the buyer's liquidation or receivership. In the buyer's administration, however, his protection is likely to be less than full. The more sophisticated forms of clauses, giving the seller rights to the proceeds of sub-sales or to new or mixed products developed from his own goods, are potentially vulnerable to being treated as registrable charges. If not properly registered, they will prove to be unenforceable. Very careful drafting is needed in order to give such clauses the greatest chance of success.

The author is grateful to John Stuart former partner at Anderson Strathern, Edinburgh for his assistance in producing this chapter.

Index

For Product Safety Concerns and Information please contact our EU representative GPSR@taylorandfrancis.com Taylor & Francis Verlag GmbH, Kaufingerstraße 24, 80331 München, Germany

Batch number: 10726007

Printed by Printforce, the Netherlands